CHAPTER ONE

"For now, we see in a dim mirror, but then face-to-face." Now I am only able to see a part of it; I will then be fully aware, just as I was fully known. 1 Corinthians

13:12 (ESV)

It's been more than twenty years since my summer spent working on an Israeli kibbutz. When I was sixteen, I thought that if I spent an additional year volunteering on the kibbutz in Israel, I would still be only 18 when I graduated from High School. It was only a few miles from Galilee's sea of Galilee that I lived, and each evening was a joy after a hot day. After dark, it would cool off and we would walk or sit around talking in small groups. I still vividly recall the time.

The first time I was brought up the subject of predestination and free will was in 2009. My immediate response was: "Why did God make us do this?" Why not just make us in heaven?

No one can really provide definitive answers to the question. This point was against this point and this Bible verse against this Bible verse. Each side claimed they were using exegesis (deriving meanings from the text) and the other was accused of eisegesis ("reading meanings into the text"). Everyone agreed that God was sovereign and that man was responsible. However, it left the question unanswered?

It would be many years before I finally read the first book on the subject. My friend started attending "Reformed Theology" church, and she sent my wife Chosen By God, by R.C. Sproul. The answers Calvinism provided to this friend were very exciting. She felt accepted by God as she is. It was all God. He chose her and she had nothing to do with it.

The book was well-received and I have read it again several times. I was not satisfied with the answers and theology in Chosen By God. Without great explanations, I disagreed. I was not only unable to feel right, but I also engaged in some seems to me theology. "It seems to be that if it is up to man to make the decision, then God is not in control." It seems to me that if everything is up to God, then God must be the author of evil. I started to read books on the subject. I could choose between zero point Calvinism or five-point Calvinism, as well as all other numbers.

When Norman Geisler's book Chosen but Free came out, I felt like I had found the answers. I finally had the answers to my questions, and was able to debate a Calvinist. Geisler explained that Calvin did not believe in a "Limited Atonement", but instead taught a "Universal Atonement". Geisler called his position "Moderate Calvinism" along with the view of Sproul. "Extreme Calvinism."

I decided to write a book to prove to my Calvinist friends, that Calvin believed in a universal atonement and that Jesus had died for all people, not just the elect. I ordered Calvin's "Institutes" as well as a set of his commentaries. I created a file on my computer, named it "Saving Calvin From Reformed Theology," and started typing Calvin quotes. For three weeks, this futility exercise was fun. I spent hours poring over Calvin trying to figure out the mysteries of sovereignty, free will and the atoning work of Christ.

Then, I found A Treatise on The Eternal Predestination Of God. This document was written by Calvin and summarises and defends his "Institutes" against attacks by Albert Pighius and Georgius (an Italian monk). I was convinced that Calvin didn't believe Jesus died for everyone. I found it hard to understand what Calvin believed as I continued reading this Treatise and Calvin's commentary. One thing was certain though: Geisler was wrong regarding Calvin, which meant that R. C. Spul was teaching.

"Classical Calvinism" and not "Extreme Calvinism" I came to the conclusion that

John Calvin taught a limited atonement and believed that all Jesus' disciples would be saved.

The Potters Freedom by James White was my next book. White confirmed many of my beliefs about Calvin. White addresses many of the Calvin quotes Geisler used in his entirety and uses almost identical reasoning to mine that convinced me Calvin taught limited atonement. (See PF. pp. 253 - 262). It is clear that each side has a deep misunderstood the other in their discussion about Calvin's limited atonement. The five points of Calvinism are discussed by most of the authors I've read: (1) Total Depravity; (2) Unconditional Election; (3) Limited Atonement; (4) Irresistible grace; (5) Perseverance Of the Saints.

One caveat: The fifth point can be wrong if the other four are incorrect. However, the fifth point could still be true if the first four are correct. This can be stated in another way: Even if one of the four points is wrong, the other four are incorrect. However, the fifth point can still be true.

There are three combinations possible:

~

First - All Five True:
Total Depravity - True
Unconditional Election - True
Limited Atonement - True
Irresistible Grace - True
The Saints' Perseverance - True

~

Second - All Five False:

Total Depravity - False

Unconditional Election - False
Limited Atonement - False
Irresistible Grace - False
Perseverance of Saints - False

~

Third - First Four True, Fifth True

Total Depravity - False
Unconditional Election - False
Limited Atonement - False
Irresistible Grace - False
The Saints' Perseverance - True

~

Also, I believe that all five points can be correct if one of the four first points is correct. This means that there can only one type of Calvinist...

This demonstrates the importance of the Limited Atonement, which Geisler used as a point of attack in his book Chosen but Free. (CBF, appendix 2, appendix 2). This view is from Moses Amyrald (a French Protestant pastor), and Calvinists refer the teachings of Amyrald as the "Amyraut Heresy." CBF, p. 56. Geisler seems to want to keep Calvin as a support for his view because he doesn't want to abandon sola gratia and sola fidei. This is just a guess based on Geisler's Systematic Theology. He states that the cry for reformation was justification through faith alone. (ST 3, p. 258)

While I was reading these books, I was having an email conversation with my friends about the same topic. I led a group to learn some of the things I had learned and tried to explain the differences between "Calvinists",

"Arminians". After reading a number of books by C. S. Lewis I was able to understand Calvin's reformed position.

Calvin and C. S. Lewis both believe in the authority and sovereignty of God and have faith in Jesus Christ. Both would affirm The Apostles Creed and The Nicene Creed. One of the most difficult problems that the reformation has created was the question of why two "protestants", looking at the same scriptures, would come up with radically different conclusions. Only after I discovered the foundational point of each man that I understood why they believed what they did, did I understand the true motivations behind their beliefs.

In the next chapters, I will try to present side-by-side the belief systems of Calvin and C. S. Lewis. I will attempt to explain each man's views and give quotes from his followers and friends to back it up. Most of what I will say is not new. I have found that both sides misrepresent arguments of the other side because they don't fully understand each other.

The study of C. S. Lewis' beliefs can help bring unity to Christ's body. As Jesus said:

"A new commandment that I give you is to love each other:

Just as I love you, so you should also love one another. This will make all people know you are My disciples if you love one another. John

13 : 34 - 35 (ESV)

I want to explain the concepts in a way that both sides can understand, regardless of their backgrounds or perspectives. I hope that you will be able to grasp the mystery of reformation and the solution through this presentation. Instead of paraphrasing Scriptures, shouting exegesis! and getting frustrated with one another, we can have a rational discussion about the real issues.

You might be like the Dwarves from "The Last Battle" (The Dwarfs for the Dwarfs! I hope you will also see the importance of these concepts and gain a deeper understanding about God. It was partly because I wanted to understand the meaning of each person's words and their motivations. I ask you to put aside any preconceived notions and "seek first understanding."

These are Abraham Joshua Heschel's great quotes that really drive home the point:
"Rather than focusing on what you see, it is important to remember the principle of knowing what you see.

It is better to know what we don't know than to see it. Instead of blaming things for being unclear, we should blame our biases and beggars of self-induced repetition. Understanding (Divine election) is more about understanding than knowledge. It is exegesis, not just understanding. It is sharing the perspective that the original understanding was made. Each mind works with presuppositions and premises, as well as a certain way of thinking. (The Prophets, intro., pp. 9-13, Abridged. I substituted "Divine Election".

"Prophecy" in the original.)
The next chapter will discuss an important area of agreement between John Calvin, C. S. Lewis.

=

CHAPTER TWO

~

"Now, there are many other things Jesus did. Were every

One of them to be published, I believe that the world could not contain all the books that would be created. John 21:25 (ESV).

Let's not be bibliophilic. The triune God is above and beyond the Scriptures. We don't worship The Bible, but we worship the God revealed through the Scriptures. The Holy Bible was inspired by the Holy Spirit and is sufficient and authoritative (2 Timothy 3:16-17). There are many books, but every sermon, and every discussion about God, is "commentary." It's all about God and His revealed Word:

MacDonald: "Sad indeed would the whole thing be, if God had told us all the Bible meant for us to believe. The Bible is greatly misunderstood. It is not the Word, Truth, or Way of God. The Bible takes us to Jesus Christ, the infinite, ever-evolving Revelation of God. Christ is the one "in whom are hidden all the treasures wisdom and knowledge." The Bible does not lead to Him. (Unspoken

Sermons, p. 18)

The Apostles creed and the Nicene creed do not appear in Scripture word for word, but they are used to'measure sticks' what is considered orthodox Christianity. It is extremely valuable to study the writings of those who have come before us in faith. It would be absurd to ignore the efforts of past generations and continue fighting over the doctrines of the trinity or the deity Christ. It's easy to find the thoughts of those who dealt with these issues, and to see how their creeds seamlessly fit with Scripture.

Scripture doesn't contain all truth about God. Scripture also doesn't contain all truth about the world. Although the Pythagorean Theorem is not in Scripture, it still holds true and is Truth. To interpret Scripture, one must be a rational being. Otherwise, one could just open the Bible and place it in front of a squirrel to see what happens. Even then, to understand the meaning of what the squirrel saw between the Scriptures and us, we'd need to be rational. We cannot read if we don't have the ability to reason. It is practically impossible to think without logic. (ST 1, p.92) Without the ability to use reason to understand the meaning of the words, you would be unable to read this sentence or the Scriptures.

We wouldn't be able to reason if we didn't have a way to live and experience the world. To be able use logic laws to reason, we must first exist as rational beings. We wouldn't be able understand what we are feeling without reason. Without reason, the sentences and words you read would not have any meaning. Experience and reason are interrelated. You are both reasoning and experiencing the words on this page.

C. S. Lewis describes the balance of logic and experience:

(Lewis) "It's Reason that teaches us to not rely solely on Reason in this matter." Reason is aware that she can't work without materials. Reason whispers to you, "Go and look!" When it becomes obvious that you can't find out whether the cat is in the linen cupboard or not, This is not my job. It is a matter for your senses. This is what we are doing. Reason cannot supply the materials to correct our abstract concept of God. She will be the first one to tell you to experience it - 'Oh, Taste and See! She will, of course, have already pointed out the absurdity in your current position. (Miracles, p. 259)

Reason is the ability to put logic to work correctly. Unreasonable people don't use logic correctly. They are ignoring logic's laws and common sense. I will certainly not argue that God is unreasonable.

Calvin and C. S. Lewis are not at odds over the use of reason and logic as the foundation of all thought. This is what they both agree to. R.C. R.C:

(Sproul) "I don't like contradictions. They are not comforting to me. They seem so easy to use that Christians are often able to do the same for me. I often hear people say that God is greater than logic. Or "Faith is greater than logic!" to defend the use contradictions in theology.

Yes, I agree with the statement that God is greater than logic and that faith is essential.

Higher than reason. With all my heart, and all my mind, I agree. I will not accept a God that is less than logic or a faith that is less than reason. A God that is less than logic should be destroyed. Irrational faith is absurd and lower than rational. (CBG, p. 40)

(Sproul:) "Christians should not embrace both poles in a blatant contradiction. This is intellectual suicide. It is also a sin to denigrate the Holy Spirit. The Holy Spirit is not the one who causes confusion. God doesn't speak with a forked tongue. (CBG, p. 41; underlined is mine).

(Sproul) "Contradictions cannot coexist, not even within the mind of God." If the truth of both sides of a true contradiction is possible in God's mind, then no revelation God has ever given us could have any meaning.

If goodness and evil, justice, injustice, righteousness, and unrighteousness could all be understood by God, then truth of any kind is impossible. (CBG, p. 44; underlined mine).

This excellent description and use logic should be embraced by all!

C. S. Lewis is a complement to R. C. Sproul:
(Lewis) "... An open mind about ultimate foundations

Ignocy is either of Theoretical Reason or Practical Reason. These things are not for him if he has his mind open. He cannot say anything about the purpose. (Abolition, p. 481)

The basic logic laws are essential for reasoning correctly. Aristotle discovered and standardized the basic laws of logic. These are some of the most fundamental laws:

1.   The law of noncontradiction: A cannot be non-A: God can not be non-God: God does not have a devil.

2.   The law of identity: A Is A: God is God.

3.   The law of the excluded middle is A or Non-A. We are referring to God or not God.

4.   The law of rational inference: Inferences can be drawn from what is known to what is not. Without this law, it is impossible to prove anything.These four points can be found in Reason, p. 16

Norman Geisler, Ronald Brooks and others share great insights into logic:

Geisler: "From the perspective of reality, it is clear that God is the foundation of all logic. All truth can be found in Him, as He is the ultimate reality. He created the world we know, and we have learned the logic laws. These laws are impossible to deny because He has created the world. However, God did not first know us and we learned logic from Him. Although He is the foundation of logic in reality, we discovered logic first, and then came to know God through it. Even if we come to know God through His revelations, this is true because logic helped us understand the revelation. God is the first in the order that He exists; however, logic allows us to know God through the order that we know. God is the foundation of logic in the order of being, but logic is the basis for all knowledge of God in the order that knowing. (Reason, page 17 - parentheses and italics in original).

Geisler: "It is true, God is superior to all other things. This means that God is above logic in the order. Logic is a type of rational thought and God is the ultimate rational Being. Logic is therefore subject to God ontologically (the study and understanding of being). This does not mean logic is arbitrarily created. God chooses to be consistent and rational. By His very nature, He is rational. Scriptures tell us that God cannot lie (Hebrews 6,18) or that He cannot deny himself (2 Timothy 2,13 NKJV). God can't be rational. It is against His nature as the supreme, perfect, and absolutely rational Being of the universe to break the laws. (ST 1, p. 90, italics in the original - "The study of Being" added for clarification)

Geisler: "Logic is the precondition for all rationality."

thought. Rational thought is what makes man different from animals and allows us to experience God. To get to Chicago, for example, I will need a map. Chicago must exist before I can use the map to help me get there. To understand God, logic is the first step. But God exists.

First, we must know Him. (Reason, p. 17)

These statements regarding logic are supported by C. S. Lewis:

(Lewis) "If you are unsure of the value or utility of your reasoning, then you should not attempt to prove it with reasoning." A proof that there is no proof is not true if it is also false. Reason is our starting point. It can be attacked or defended in any way you like. You can't treat it as a phenomenon if you try to get inside it. (Miracles p.222 - my underlined - "Beginning the question" is an illogical fallacy that will be explained in the next chapter.

Geisler: "While God is before logic in the order to be"

Ontologically, logic is before God in the order for knowing.

(epistemologically). The laws of thought are essential for knowledge. If this is false, then no other information will follow. The statement "God exists" is meaningless if the law of identity (A is A) is true. The affirmation that God exists cannot be true if it is impossible to prove the law of noncontradiction. Otherwise, God could exist simultaneously and in the same way. (ST 1, p.90 - quotation marks and parentheses in original).

The following quote is a truth of great value to me. It is worth taking the time to read it slowly. Enjoy the beauty of it. We will return to it down the road if it is not clear to you now. When the opposing views are presented, I think you'll be able to see the value in this concept:

Geisler: "This doesn't make God subject to anything beyond Himself. God is only subject to logic (good reason), but He is also subject to His nature (see Clark and CVMT), as He is the ultimate Reason (John 1:1). The law of justice is the same. God is not bound to anything outside Himself. He is only bound to His unchangeable nature. (ST 1, p. 91)

Geisler explains why logic is important in God's study:

Geisler: "God is author of all logic." Technically, this is true.

Logic flows from God, but God doesn't flow from logic. Our statements about God are what we should be examining using logic. Nobody is trying to determine God. Logic analyzes the statements and "commentary" we make about Him. Logic is a tool that allows us to verify whether these statements are true and if they correspond with the reality of God's character. Theology uses logic to test our beliefs about God.

God has a way for us all to find the truth. (Reason, pp. 17 - 18)

Geisler: Systematic Theology is a collection of statements about God which, if true inform us about Him. If it does not follow the unavoidable rules of reason, no statement about God is likely to make sense. (ST 1, p. 91)

Logical study does not only focus on correct reasoning. It also includes many fallacies. Petitio Principii is an example of a logic fallacy, which can be translated as "begging the question":

Geisler: "This argument is where the conclusion is sneaked

In the premises. "Accept this conclusion because the premise from where it comes is true." This is a circular argument in which the conclusion becomes a preposition. (Reason, p. 100)

One example of "begging the questions" is that the Bible states that:

"All Scripture is inspired by God and is profitable

doctrine, for correction, and instruction in righteousness. 2 Timothy 3 : 16 (KJV)

The Bible must then be true:
Geisler: "By referring the Bible as proof there is an implicit

Assumption that the Bible is divinely inspired. That is precisely the question being asked. It's not enough to say the Bible says it was from God. The Koran (and the Book of Mormon) also support this assertion. This assumption premise reaffirms the conclusion and raises the question. (Reason, page 100 - the parenthetical statement was mine.

This does not necessarily mean that the Bible lies, but that one argument used in it is false. You can find many more fallacies in logic books. The one I have been quoting is: Come Let Us Reason by Brooks and Geisler.

Geisler provides a great summary:
Geisler: "All Truth is revealed to us by God in special or general revelations, but we can only receive the truth by reason." (ST 1, p. 91 – italics in the original) "While there are some objections to logic, there is a distinction between the use good reason, which Scripture recommends for discovering truth (Isaiah 1:18 and Matthew 22:37, 1 Peter 3:15) and the use rationalism to determine truth. Scripture doesn't recommend this. Good reason doesn't subject God to finite thoughts, but instead subjects our finite minds and His

infinite Mind to it. (2 Cor. 10:5; 1 Cor. 1:21)." "(ST 1, p.91 - my addition is in italics in original underlined words)

These verses illustrate how Scripture and Reason can be combined to reach the right conclusion:

> Matthew 19:26 Jesus looked at them, and said, "With man."

This is impossible, but God makes all things possible. " (ESV)

> Luke 1:37 "For God is not able to do anything." (ESV)

> Hebrews 6:18 "...it is impossible to God lie ...""
(ESV).

It is evident that lying is a phenomenon. Since all things are possible for God it would seem obvious that God could lie. However, this contradicts Scripture, which clearly states that God cannot lie. It is difficult for God to lie about a thing, but God can do anything?

John 14:6 Jesus told him that he was the truth and the way.

life. I am the only way to get to God. (ESV)

It is impossible for God to be both truthful and lieful. It is impossible for a being to be both truthful and lieful. It is absurd to say such a being exists. It is absurd to say that such a being could exist. Scripture says that God can do all things. It is also true that God is capable of doing anything. A being that is simultaneously a liar or the truth is absurd, and it is therefore not real.

The next chapter will discuss the foundational beliefs of Calvin, C. S. Lewis, and how logic is used to extract a particular meaning.

Scripture. Both C. S. Lewis and Calvin agree on the early creeds

Each Christian has a different view on God's attributes.

Omnipotence refers to Adam's original sin and Eve's first sin. Each man uses

Scripture and reason can both lead to a conclusion. These are two opposing conclusions

These are the foundation of each man's systematic religion. Each systemic theology is almost in complete contradiction to the other. It is impossible to reconcile them.

=

CHAPTER THREE

~

"The LORD does whatever He pleases in heaven and earth.

In the seas and deeps." Psalms 135 :6 (ESV).

&

"Our God is in heaven; He does whatever He pleases." Psalms, 115:3

(ESV)

&

"For God is not impossible." Luke 1:37 (NIV).

Surprised to discover that Calvin and C. S. Lewis both have these verses as the foundation of their belief on Soteriology (salvation). It is quite easy to see the problem: If God is Omnipotent and Good, then why did Adam and Lucifer sin? Either God is unable to eliminate evil or he wants but cannot. Or he could, but he doesn't want to. He is ineffective if he does not want to but cannot. He is evil if he cannot and doesn't want to. If God can and will abolish evil, how then is evil allowed to enter the world? "Theodicy" refers to attempts to solve this problem.

First, I will outline the theodicy that "Classical Calvinism", or "Reformed Theology," uses to solve this problem. Then, I build on this foundation to systematize other aspects of the Calvinistic view about Soteriology. I will use Calvin quotes or others that accurately reflect the Calvinist view to help me let the Calvinist position speak for myself. I will either provide a brief introduction to the quotes or summarize the conclusions that can easily be drawn from them.

R.C. R.C:

(Sproul) "If God is completely righteous, then how could he have created an environment where evil is present?" Isn't evil also a result of God if all things are created by him? I saw that evil was a problem within the sovereignty of God. Is evil a threat to God's sovereignty?

sovereign will? If He does not, then He is not absolute sovereign. If so, we can conclude that God has foreordained evil in some way. (CBG, pp. 28-29 - italics in the original

(Sproul) "We hear a lot of objections that God created us because He knew we would sin. The problem was described by a philosopher as "If God knew that we would sin, but couldn't stop it," then He is neither omnipotent or sovereign. If He could have stopped it, but chose not to do so, then He is neither loving or benevolent. This approach makes God look bad, no matter what we answer.

It is reasonable to assume that God knew ahead of time that man would fall. It is possible that God could intervene to stop it. Or He could choose not to

create us. All of these possibilities are possible. (CBG, 32 - Underline mine)
To sum up R.C. Sproul:

1. An Omniscient God could predict in advance when man will fall.

2. A Omnipotent God could have stopped the fall.

3. The Perfect God wouldn't need to create man. Calvin agrees with Sproul on the first point, that an Omniscient God would see that man would fall:

(Calvin) "God foresaw Adam's fall, and most definitely His

Allowing him to fall was not against, but in accordance with, His Divine will!"

(EPG, p. 76)
Calvin agrees with Sproul on the first and second points in the following quote:

that an Omniscient God knew Adam would fall, and an Omnipotent God could have stopped Adam from falling:

Calvin: "And if the matter is carried higher and a question about the first creation of men be raised, Augustine responds by saying: "We most wholesomely admit, that which was rightly believed: That God, the Lord, created all things 'very well' and foreknew that evil would arise from it: And He also knew that it was more to His glory to bring good out evil than to allow evil to exist at all!" (EPG, p. 25, underlined by me)

Here's a second quote from Calvin, where Calvin says that an Omnipotent God could stop the fall of Adam:

(Calvin) "Therefore, as far these natures were concerned, their actions were contrary to God's will. But, as far the omnipotence God is concerned they acted in accordance with His will. They could not have done so contrary to it." (EPG, p. 26. Original underline mine.

Augustine is again quoted by Calvin. They explain that their theology rests on the assumption that God knew Adam would die and that God could stop Adam from sin:

Calvin: "Evil things are not good in the sense that they are bad. But it is good that there should be both good and evil things. If there was this good, then evil things would not exist. Without a doubt, He can just as easily refuse to allow what He doesn't want to be done as He can do what He wants to. If we don't believe this, our faith will be ruined from the beginning. In other words, we believe in God ALMAIGHTY! (EPG, pp. 25 - 26 – underline mine - Capitalization & italics in the original

Although Sproul stated that God could intervene to stop the fall, Augustine & Calvin explain how God might have done so: By overruling Adam's disobedience.

Anselm of Canterbury, around the year 1070 wrote that God was "that beyond which nothing greater could be conceived." One example is that God has all power, which is the most power man can imagine God having. Therefore, God is Omnipotent. God can only be imagined to have all-knowing, the greatest amount of knowledge one could imagine. Therefore, God is Omniscient. This reasoning can be applied to many attributes of God. However, for Calvin's Theology, the most important attributes are Omnipotence, Freedom, or Liberty.

Anselm's proposition states that God is the most liberated being. Therefore, God has the greatest freedom of all beings, and God is also the most free-willing being we can imagine. This freedom is often expressed in Calvin's theology as Sovereignty.

(Calvin) "But it would be absurd to hold that anything could be done against the will of God; since God is at Divine liberty prevent what He doesn't will be done." Augustine shows, with this argument, that all that is done on Earth is effectively governed and overruled by the secret providence God. He also concludes that all that is done is due to the

WILL OF GOD! The Psalmist supports this conclusion.

God, sitting in heaven does what He will. "But our God (saith The

The Psalmist is in heaven: He has done whatever He pleases." (Ps.

155:3.)" (EPG, page 190 - capitalization and italics in original)

Calvin says that God, being Omnipotent, Sovereign, is free to decide or overrule any decision or act of His creatures at any given time. If God does not choose to over-rule His creatures, then God allows the decision or action to be made. Calvin quotes Augustine: "Nothing is done but that which the Omnipotent willed, either by permitting it or by doing it himself." (EPG, p. 25, italics in the original)

Calvin: "God doesn't just allow a thing to happen or continue because of His patience, but He also rules and overrules what is done."

His All-powerful power." (EPG, p. 60; underlined is mine).

God had the power to overrule Adam's sin. God, therefore, must have allowed Adam to sin. This is a repeat of Augustine and Calvin: "For, except there was this good, that evil things also existed. Those evil things would not be allowed to exist by the Great and Good Omnipotent. Without a doubt, He can just as easily refuse to allow what He doesn't want to be done as He can do what He wants to. This is the danger to our faith from the beginning. We believe in God ALMAIGHTY, but we don't believe it fully. (EPG, pp. 25-26 underlined is mine.

Calvin begins with "the very beginning" of our faith and teaches these six points:

1.   God must have the power to overrule all His creatures' decisions at all times. Otherwise, God is not Omnipotent or Sovereign.Calvin: "Therefore, we can rest assured that no human will can resist God's will. He does all things in heaven and earth according to His will; and who already has done the things that will be done by His will. We repeat: No human will can stop God from doing what He wants. He does what He wills with all the wills of mankind. (EPG, p. 134)

2.   Adam and Eve had free-will (points #3 and #4 define "free-will")(Calvin) "He so preordained the lives angels and men that He

They might be the first to show what free-will can do in them." (EPG, p. 25)

(Calvin) "He fell on his own free-will and his own initiative.

Willing to act." (EPG, p. 76)

(Sproul) "Calvinism is Adam's sin by his free will,

Not by divine coercion." (CBG, p. 97)

3.   Adam and Eve received free-will as a gift.(Sproul) "Free-will" is a good thing. God gave us free will

He is not to be blamed. Man was created with the ability to sin and the ability not to sin. (CBG, p. 30)

(Calvin:) (agrees to Pighius: "God wished for a rational world."

capable of receiving this goodness from God. This could not have been done without His giving that creature freedom of choice. (EPG, p. 70)

4.   Free-will refers to the ability to sin or not to sin. Adam was created with free-will. He is "perfectly upright," with the light of reason, and with the rectitude of his nature.(Calvin) "I have always asserted that man was created in,"

The beginning is perfectly upright." (EPG, p. 112)

(Calvin:) Adam was perfect and could do it perfectly. (EPG, p. 114)

(Calvin) "Man was adorned in order that he might be the Image of God."

From the first with the light and rectitude of the natural world. (EPG, p.

71 - Rectitude - Rightness of principle, conduct, moral virtue. Correctness: Straightness.

5.   Sin was the fall. Sin is evil. The fall was an evil event.Romans 5:12 says that sin was brought into the world by one man (ESV).

(Sproul:) "sin...is evil" (CBG, p. 31)

Calvin: "For we know that nothing is more contrary than the

Nature of God is better than sin. (EPG, p. 187)

6.   The test of obedience was the tree of knowledge of good or evil. Adam and Eve had free-will but were still subject to the control of God. God gave Adam and Eve free will by giving them the knowledge tree of good and bad.

                    (Calvin) "Therefore the prohibition of one Tree was a
          Test of

  obedience." (Genesis, p. 125 - 126)

(Calvin:) "Therefore abstinence was required from one tree's fruit.

  As a first lesson in obedience, a man might realize he had a Director or Lord in his life. He should be able to trust in his will and obey those who direct him. (Genesis, p. 126)

                    (Calvin) "But at which time we speak, a principle
          was

  Given to man so that he could know that God ruled over his life. (Commentary on Genesis p. 126)

                    (Calvin:) "Therefore, when God commands Adam to
          not taste

  The fruit of the "tree knowledge of good or evil"; he thereby tests his obedience. (EPG, p. 185)

     Here are the six points, without any supporting quotes:
  1. God must have the power to overrule all His creatures' decisions at all times. Otherwise, God is not Omnipotent or Sovereign.
  2. Adam and Eve had "free will".
  3. Adam and Eve received free-will as a gift.

4. Free-will refers to the ability to sin or not to sin.

5. Sin was the fall. Sin is evil. The fall was an evil event.

6. The test of obedience was the tree of knowledge of good or evil.Scripture clearly reveals that Adam sinned and disobeyed God. He did evil, and fell:

(Calvin) "But it would be absurd to hold that anything could be done against the will of God; since God is at Divine liberty prevent what He doesn't will be done." "...Augustine demonstrates... that all that is done on Earth is effectively ruled and overruled by the secret providence God! He also concludes that all that is done is due to the WILL OF GOD! (EPG, p. 190).

The fall of Adam must have occurred according to God's secret providence and will:

Calvin: "Augustine testifies that God, in secret and marvellous ways, justly wills the things which men do unjustly. " (EPG, p. 179)

(Calvin) "God foresaw Adam's fall, and most definitely His

Allowing him to fall was not against, but in accordance with, His Divine will!"

(EPG, p. 76)

An Omnipotent God might have prevented Adam and Eve from sin. This is because an Absolutely Sovereign Omnipotent God can overrule Adam and Eve's decision. Since an Omniscient God would know men will sin, an Omnipotent God can stop Adam from sinning, and a Perfect God does not need to create man.

Below is a chart that illustrates what Augustine (and Calvin) call the "very beginning of our faith":

To illustrate how Reformed Theology is an interconnected system of belief, the points placed between the dotted lines throughout the book will be used. Additional points will be made as the discussion continues:

Reformed Theology Foundation / Calvinism:

    1. God can overrule the decisions of any of His creatures.

      2. A. God is OmniscientB. God is OmnipotentC.

    3. A. God knew that the fall would occur.

4.   God could have prevented the fallGod didn't have to create anything.The fall was willed, preordained and decreed by God.--------------------

Reformed Theology can be described as a systematic Theology. It is interconnected from end to end. It can be described as a braided rope. The rope's threads are intertwined, and cannot be separated from each other. The rope can only be untied from one end, so we see ends of rope being burned to fuse them together. It is essential to make sure that your theological system has a solid foundation. While I do not claim that your foundation is correct,

Reformed Theology holds that Adam and Eve could not have sinned if there was an Omnipotent God -- Augustine and Calvin are all saying this. They say this is the right place to start. This is where you should start. C. S. Lewis would also agree that this is a good place to start.

Let's look at these three foundational statements by using the laws we agreed to in the last chapter. The following structure is used: A rational being experiences God, as revealed in Scriptures. We call this "Theology" truth statements about God that we draw from this revelation. These theological statements are used by man to create a "philosophy". These meaning statements are examined by Logic / Reason in order to determine if they're Orthodox beliefs or correct thinking.

    1. The Calvinists believe that God is Omniscient. This means God knew that sin would happen. God cannot be Omniscient if he didn't know that man would sin. God knew ahead of time that man would sin.

2. The Calvinists believe that God is Omnipotent. This means God could have stopped man from sin. God cannot have stopped man from sinning if God does not have the power to do so. All that happens is God's will and man must have sinned because God made it so.

3. The Calvinists believe that God is perfect. This means God didn't need to create man. God does not need to create if God is perfect without His creation. God could have chosen to not create man. These three propositions are what Augustine and Calvin call the "beginning of faith", while R.C. These propositions are simply called assumptions by Sproul. These men are right when they say that Calvinism is built on these three philosophical presuppositions. This quote was taken from a conference where R. C. Sproul and Albert Mohler were answering questions from the audience. Sproul will present a summary on the origins of evil and use the second principle outlined above:

(Sproul) "When evil enters the world through God's design

God's sovereign will makes evil evil. It is a sin for people to call evil good or evil evil. But when God orders evil to occur, it's good. God is all-good and only ordains what is good. It is bad that evil exists, but He wouldn't allow it to be. This isn't too difficult. (Sproul, National Conference 2007, 2007)

This explanation is compatible with Augustine's previous quote:

"And He also knew that it was more to His glory."

Omnipotent goodness, to bring out the best in evil than to allow evil to exist at all! (EPG, p. 25)

Martin Luther also agrees and appeals to logic/reason as proof that his foundational view is correct:

(Luther) "For if it is true, God foreknows all things; He cannot be deceived or hindered in His Prescience, predestination, and that everything can happen only according to His Will (which reason herself is forced to admit;) then even according to reason's testimony, there can be no free will --in man, angel, or in any creature! (Bondage p. 390; my underlined is mine).

Augustine, Luther and Calvin are united in their view of God's fall and that of man. Calvinism is more than just the five "TULIP" points. These are the foundation of Calvin's systematic theology. This foundation is the basis for the traditional five points of Calvinism. This foundation is the "original understanding" from which it is built. Before I show you how the rest of Calvinism can be built upon this foundation, let me explain how C. S. Lewis views the same scriptures in a different way. This leads to a opposing foundation. First, I'll list the scriptures starting at the beginning of this chapter:

"The LORD does whatever He pleases in heaven and earth.

In the seas and deeps. Psalms 135 :6 (ESV).

"Our God is in heaven; He does whatever He pleases." Psalms: 115:3 (ESV).

"For God is not impossible." Luke 1:37 (NIV).

There are many scriptures that deal with the same topic, but they also show that God cannot do certain things, or that God is unable to do them:

"When God wanted to prove more convincingly to his heirs the unchangeable nature of his purpose, He made an oath to do so. We who fled for safety might find strong encouragement to keep the faith we have in God. Hebrews 6:17-18 (ESV - underline mine) God's eyes are too pure for evil. God cannot see evil and overlook wrong:

"Are your not from everlasting O LORD my God, My Holy One?"?

We will not die. O LORD, you have given them to you as a judgement, and you, O Rock have made them for reproof. If you have purer eyes than can see evil and can't look at wrong, then why do your blinders look at traitors while the wicked swallows up those who are more righteous?

he?" Habakkuk 1:12-13 (ESV – underlined mine)

God cannot deny Himself:

"The saying is true, for: If He has died with us, we will also live together with Him; and if He suffers, He will also reign with us. If we deny Him, He will also deny our faithlessness. He is faithful, because He cannot deny Himself. 2 Timothy 2:11-13 (ESV-underline mine) God is not capable of being tempted by evil and God cannot tempt men:

"Let no person say, when tempted," "I am being temped by God." God is not capable of being tempted with evil and He Himself does not tempt anyone. James 1:13 (ESV, underline mine)

We can return to Anselm's assertion, which Calvin and C. S. Lewis both agree with: God has the greatest freedom of all beings. God is therefore the most liberated being. God is also the freest being that we can conceive.

If God must have the ability to rule over any of His creatures' actions or decisions at any time, then God can do anything but give freedom to His creatures. Calvin's view on the freedom and Omnipotence Gods leads to the conclusion God can do anything but give His creatures real freedom. This means that God cannot give His creatures real freedom. Anselm's assertion that God is "that beyond which nothing greater could be imagined" is correct. God, therefore, is the most free Being. God, as such, is free to grant real freedom to His creatures.

Calvin's first point was made at the beginning:

1. God is the most liberated being or God is more free than men. God must be able to rule over all His creatures' decisions, otherwise God isn't Omnipotent or Sovereign.

(Sproul) "I once saw a statement from a Christian that said, "God is my shepherd."

Human freedom can't be restricted by sovereignty." Imagine a Christian thinker saying such a thing. This is pure humanism. (CBG, p. 42)

Argument: God can stop any man at anytime from doing any thing, or God is not sovereign. God can stop any man from doing any thing at any moment, but man is more free that God.

If God can't stop man, it means that man is doing something God cannot stop. This is a sign that God isn't sovereign and God is reacting to him.

(Sproul) "God is Free. I am free. God is freer than I am. If

My freedom is limited by God's freedom. I lose. His freedom is restricted by mine, but my freedom is not. (CBG, p. 43)

This is Sproul's argument. He argues that Adam could not sin if God didn't intervene.

1. This is the first presupposition philosophically of Reformed Theology:

God can do whatever He pleases, but God cannot give any freedom to His creatures.

OR

1. God cannot give any freedom to His creatures since God would not be completely Sovereign.

This philosophical presupposition is contrary to points 2, 3 & 4.

All three of these teachers are Augustine, Calvin, and Sproul. (2. Adam and Eve had free will. 3. Adam and Eve received free-will as a gift. 4. (Free-will refers to the ability or inability to sin. This philosophical assumption is also against Scripture. Specifically, Gen 2:6-17, where Scripture says that God can give real freedoms to His creatures. God gave real freedom to Adam when He told him that he could eat from any tree.

C. S. Lewis would agree to all six points of Calvin, except for the first. The first point would be:

1. God, as Sovereign of His creation, is free to grant real freedom to His creatures. He did this in Genesis 2:16-17.

The following Chapter 2 is from "The Problem of Pain", by C. S. Lewis. The chapter title is "DIVINE OMNIPOTENCE". C. S. Lewis will present his case using a short quotation from Saint Thomas Aquinas, and four simple paragraphs:

(Lewis) "Nothing that implies contradiction is under the omnipotence God. THOMAS AQUINAS. Summ. Theol.

ART 4"

(Lewis)

All creatures are happy and God would grant them all their wishes. The creatures, however, are unhappy. The problem with pain is that God does not have either goodness or power or both. It is possible to answer it if we show that the terms good' and 'almighty', as well as the term happy' are equivocal. For it must be acknowledged from the beginning that if these popular meanings are the best or only possible meanings then the argument cannot be answered. This chapter will discuss the concept of Omnipotence and the following some thoughts on the idea that Goodness is possible.

(Lewis) "Omnipotence" means "power to do everything or all". The original Latin meaning of "power over or in all" may have been "power over or in all". This is what I believe to be the current meaning. Scripture tells us that all things are possible with God. In argument with unbelievers, it is not uncommon to hear that God, if He existed, would do this or that. Then, when we say that the proposed action is impossible to accomplish, the reply is 'But I thought God was supposed be able to do everything'. This brings up the question of impossible.

(Lewis) "In normal usage, the word impossible generally means a suppressed clause that begins with the word unless. It is impossible for me see the street from my current position. I must go to the top floor to be able to see the building in front of me. If my leg was broken, I would say "But it's impossible to climb up to the top floor" -- meaning that I will need to be accompanied by friends. Let's now move to another level of impossibility. I would say "It is impossible to see the street as long as I stay where I am and any intervening buildings remain where they are." Although I don't know what the greatest scientists and philosophers would say, I'd have to respond that I don't know if space or vision could have been of such an extreme nature as you suggest. Because I don't know if it is contradictory or not, I can't say whether seeing around corners is possible in this new sense. It is impossible if it is selfcontradictory, I know this. It may also be called intrinsically impossible, because it has its own impossibility instead of borrowing from other impossibilities that depend on it. It does not have an "unless" clause. It is impossible for all circumstances and all worlds, and for all agents.

(Lewis) "All agents" here includes God Himself. His

Omnipotence is the ability to do everything that is intrinsically possible. It does not mean power to do anything that is impossible. He may be credited with miracles, but you cannot attribute nonsense to Him. There is no limit to His power. You cannot say that God can give free will to a creature and withhold it from its will. This is a false statement about God. Meaningless words don't suddenly gain meaning if we add the words "God can". All things are possible for God. The intrinsic impossibilities of God are not things, but nonentities. It is impossible for God to perform both of these mutually exclusive options. This is not because His power meets obstacles, but because nonsense continues to be nonsense even when it's about God. (POP, pp. (POP, pp. 379 - 38 - italics are in original - mine underline)

C. S. Lewis is in agreement with Calvinists about God's Omniscient, Omnipotent and Perfect nature. Lewis uses scripture to challenge the Calvinist founding assumption that an Omnipotent God could intervene to stop the fall. This would imply that God can do what is logically inconsistent. Genesis 2:6-17 addresses the question of God granting man freedom in the garden:

Genesis 2:6-17: "And the LORD God ordered the man.

"Say, Thou mayest freely eat from any tree in the garden: But, of the tree of knowledge of good or evil, thou shall not eat thereof: for the day that it is eaten, thou will surely die." (KJV)

Genesis 2:6-17: "And the LORD God ordered the man.

It is said, "You can eat from every tree in the garden, but you will not eat from the tree of knowledge of good or evil, for you will surely die if you eat it." (ESV)

Genesis 2:6-17 "And the LORD God said to the man, "You can eat from any tree within the garden, but you must not eat the tree of knowledge of good or evil. For you will surely die if you do." (NIV)

Calvin and C. S. Lewis may disagree about the first point but they are in agreement on points 2 – 6:

Calvin: 1. God, being Omnipotent, is able over-rule the decisions and actions of any of His creatures. God can do whatever He pleases, but His creatures cannot be over-ruled by Him.

Lewis: 1. God, Omnipotent, is free to grant real freedom to His creatures. He did this in Genesis 2:16-17.

Calvin & Lewis agree on 2. Adam and Eve had free-will.

3.   Adam and Eve received free-will as a gift.

4.   Free-will refers to the ability to sin or not to sin.

5.   Sin was the fall. Sin is evil. The fall was an evil event.

6. The test of obedience was the tree of knowledge of good or evil. Adam and Eve had free will, but were still subject to the control of God. God gave Adam and Eve free will by giving them the tree of knowledge of good or evil. Three questions or considerations need to be answered at this point:

1. God stopped Abimelech sinning so why wouldn't He stop Adam sinning too?

2. Was God trying to stop Adam sinning?

3.   Can God have stopped Adam sinning from the beginning? Question 1: If God stopped Abimelech sinning, then could He have stopped Adam sinning as well?

Abraham traveled from there to the Negeb, lived between Shur and Kadesh, and then he settled in Gerar.

Abraham also said to Sarah, his wife, "She's my sister." Abimelech, king of Gerar, sent Sarah.

In a nightly dream, God appeared to Abimelech and said, "Behold, your dead man because you took the woman, for she's a man's wife."

Abimelech did not approach her. He said, "Lord! Will you kill innocent people?"?

Is it possible that he did not say to me, "She is my sister"? She said it herself, "He is my brother." This was done with the integrity of my heart, and with the innocence of mine hands.

In a dream, God told him, "Yes, Lord, you did this in your integrity, and I kept you from sining against me." So I didn't let you touch her. Genesis 20:1 - 6 (ESV)

God didn't tell Abimelech that God allowed him to be with Sarah. God did tell Adam that he could eat from the tree containing the knowledge of Good or Evil.

Calvin and C. S. Lewis agreed on five points that apply to Adam. They don't apply to Abimelech. A comparison of an un-fallen Adam with a postfall Abimelech would be a weak analogy. It is a common 'category error' to compare Abimelech from the category for fallen creatures with Adam and Eve from the category for un-fallen creatures. It is important not to confuse the rules' that apply to fallen creatures with the rules that apply unfallen creatures.

C. S. Lewis agrees to R. C. Sproul's statement that "prefall man could sin" and "prefall man couldn't sin." CBG, p. 66. C. S. Lewis addresses this issue by writing: "If you choose the statement 'God can give a creation free will while at the same withhold free will form it', then you are not able to say anything about God."

God said that man could eat from all trees, but to stop man from eating from any tree would have made God a fool since man wouldn't have been truly free to eat off any tree. It would be logically contradictory to claim that God could allow man to eat from the trees and then refuse to give it to him.

Logically contradictory is the assertion that God granted man freedom from eating from the tree and then God ordered or directed man to eat from it.

Calvin says Adam was created in the beginning perfectly upright. Sproul also agrees that Adam was created with the ability to sin and not sin.

Calvin then tells us that God intended for the fall to occur: "But it couldn't be otherwise, Adam couldn't but fall; according the foreknowledge and will of God." (EPG, p. 76)

(Sproul) "We know God is sovereign because God is God. We must therefore conclude that God has foreordained sin. We can only conclude this conclusion. (CBG, p. 31)

What happened to free will and the ability not to sin?

(Lewis:) "not even Omnipotence can do what is self-contradictory." (Miracles, p. 241)

It is contradictory for God to give Adam the ability sin, and then to say that God can withhold that ability from Adam in the same way and at the same time.

It is paradoxical to claim that God gave Adam the "ability NOT to sin" and then to later say that God withheld Adam's "ability not to sin" at the same moment and in the exact same way. Calvin is proving exactly this when he says that Adam could not but fall, according to God's foreknowledge and will. It is paradoxical to claim that God gave Adam "rectitude in nature" and "free will", and then to suggest that God would still be able to rule Adam's actions and decisions.

Question 2: Was God trying to stop Adam sinning?

Genesis 2:27 explains that God instructed Adam not to eat from the tree of knowledge of good or evil.

Leviticus 19-18 is the first of many instances in which God commands us to love our neighbor as ourselves.

Ephesians 5 :25 - God commands that husbands love their wives just like Christ loved the church, and gave Himself for her.

It seems reasonable to draw a conclusion from Scripture that, if God intended Adam to sin then I would also need to conclude that God desires me to hate my neighbor as well as my wife. God instead commands Adam not to sin and tells us to love our spouse and neighbor. God didn't want Adam to sin. He also doesn't want you to hate and beat your wife.

Question 3: If God didn't want Adam to obey Him, could God have prevented Adam from sin?

God said to Adam that he could eat from any tree. This is how God gave Adam the gift of free-will and established the test of obedience. God would have to lie to Adam and tell him that Adam was allowed to eat from any tree. Then withhold this freedom from Adam. This is not an insult to the Omnipotence God. It is impossible for Omnipotence to do what is logically contradictory. Omnipotence cannot give and withhold freewill simultaneously.

These six points can be supported both by Scripture and Reason. These six points will be agreed upon and it will become clear that God cannot stop Adam from sin after Genesis 2:6-17. If you can't stop something from happening, knowing that it is coming to pass does not make it your responsibility. To say that the sun rose this morning through our "permissive will" would be to suggest that we could have prevented it from happening. I did not give permission for the sun's rise this morning, nor did God grant permission for Adam to sin. Contrary to Scripture, it is not possible to believe that God intended Adam to sin. God could have stopped Adam sinning or Adam sinned according God's will.

Calvin says: Sin was the fall. Sin is evil. The fall was an evil event. God could have "willed" that the fall would occur, but God did not intend for evil to happen. Calvin taught that God wills evil to occur: "God in a secret, marvellous manner justly wills the things which men unjustly make." "Even though God and Satan will do the same thing, they do it in a completely different way." (EPG, page 182 - italics original)

Luther says that "nothing can happen but according to His Will." Calvin agrees, saying: "Nothing is done but what is thee."

Omnipotent could make it happen, either by allowing it to be done or by making it happen Himself. (EPG, 25 - italics original)

Luther and Calvin believed that evil can only happen if God wills it.

1.   God willed and foreordained the fall.
2.   The fall was evil.
1.   God has allowed evil to occur:If God allows evil to occur.
2.   (And) God's will is good.
3.   Then evil is good.

I'd rather agree with Scripture and say that the forbidden fruit from the tree of knowledge of good or evil was not the permissible fruit. Adam sinned against God's command and will, and not God's permission or permissive will.

Remember chapter 2, where R. C. Sproul said: "Christians should embrace both poles in a blatant contradiction. This is intellectual suicide. It is also a slander of the Holy Spirit. The Holy Spirit is not the one who causes confusion. God doesn't speak with a forked tongue." (CBG, p. 41 underlined is mine).

Reformed theology, which teaches Adam was given the good gift of free will and rectitude by God, also implies that God could have overruled Adam's free choices. This is a clear contradiction.

This contradictory belief system leads to Reformed Theology, which teaches that all that happens is God's will. Since evil has happened and is still happening, God will cause it to happen. God wants evil to occur, and God wills good things to happen; Therefore, evil can be good. R. C. Sproul was correct. Embracing two poles in a blatant contradiction can lead to intellectual suicide as well as slander of Holy Spirit. It also leads to the slandering of God the Father, teaching that God sees evil as good. Calvinism ultimately rests on the assumption that "It seems": It seems to be that an

An Omnipotent God could have overruled Adam's decision not to sin. Calvinism, instead of "Sola Scriptura," is reduced to a manmade religion based upon "It seems so to me" theology. Calvinism insists that God must always have the power to rule His creatures. This makes God less free to grant any real freedom to His creatures.

Contrast the truth with an opposing argument that has been proven to be incorrect to make it easier to grasp. We can still use the mistakes of Reformed theology, which helps us to see the true origin of evil as well as the Sovereignty and sovereignty of God, because God is always working to make good out of bad.

Foundation of Classical Theism:
   1. God can give His creatures freedom at will.
   2. A. God is OmniscientB. God is Omnipotent
      C.   God is Perfect

3. A. God knew that the fall would occur.

4.   The fall could not be stopped by God.God didn't have to create anything.The fall wasn't ordained by God. God gave man the power to choose.--------------------

Calvin quotes Augustine's "Manual", to Laurentius, where Augustine states: "How certain, how immutable and how all-efficacious God's will is: - how many things He could or has the power to do that He won't do.": (But that He wills nothing He does not have the power to do). (EPG, p. 25,) C. S. Lewis agrees to Augustine and Aquinas that God cannot do anything logically contradictory. "His Omnipotence" means that God has the power to do everything that is intrinsically possible. It does not mean that He can do all that is intrinsically impossible. He may be credited with miracles, but you cannot attribute nonsense to him. There is no limit to His power. (POP, p. 380).

1.   S. Lewis is in agreement with Calvinists about the attributes of Omniscience,Perfection. The difference is in the meaning of what an Omnipotent God could do. C. S. Lewis doesn't agree that God could have prevented sinners from being able to sin. That would be logically contradictory.God gave man both the freedom and the ability not to sin.

2. God cannot prevent sinful behavior if man is free from sin. Satan presented the opportunity to sin.C. S. Lewis does not believe that God willed or ordained the fall of man. This would imply that God did something logically contradictory:

1. God gave man both the freedom and the ability not to sin.

2. God cannot make man sin if man is free from sin.Next, I will examine the meaning C. S. Lewis derives from the attribute Omnipotence. This paragraph uses the same structure as the beginning of this chapter to examine the beliefs of Augustine, Luther and Calvin on Omniscience, Omnipotence and Perfection:

C. S. Lewis says in scripture that God is Omnipotent. God granted man the right to eat from any tree in Genesis. This means that man could eat from any tree and God couldn't prevent it. God gave freedom to man, but withheld it from him in the same way. It was not God's will that Lucifer fell and man fall. This was against God's will. His power did not meet an immovable object. Lucifer, however, abused the power He gave them. God decreed that Lucifer, and man, were "free", but they weren't "free" from His sovereign control. God didn't "ordain" Lucifer and man to sin. Here are some quotes from C. S. Lewis about the fall: C. S. Lewis discusses his view of the fall as well as free-will in the man:

(Lewis) "God created all things that had free-will." This is what it means

There are creatures that can either go wrong or right. People think they can picture a creature that is free, but has no chance of going wrong. I cannot. A thing that is good is also good is not free to be bad. Evil is possible because of free-will. Then, why did God grant them free-will? Free-will is the only thing that allows for evil, but it also makes it possible to have love, goodness, or joy. It would be difficult to create a world of robots, or creatures that work like machines. God's higher creatures will find happiness in being voluntarily and freely united with Him. This is a joy unlike the love that is most passionate between man and woman on earth. They must be free for this.

(Lewis) "Of Course God knew what would happen to them if they used

Their freedom in the wrong direction: He seemed to think it was worth the risk. Maybe we are inclined to disagree. There is a problem with disagreeing with God. God is the source of all your reasoning power. You could not be right or He wrong, just as a stream cannot rise above its source. If you argue against Him, you are fighting against the very power that allows you to argue. It is like cutting off the branch on which you sit. If God considers that this state of war in our universe is a price worth paying to make a living world where creatures can do real harm or good and real important things can happen, then we might take it. C. S. Lewis discusses how God can prevent the fall:

(Lewis) "We might be able to imagine a world where God corrects the abuse of His free-will by His creations at every moment. So that a wooden beam was softened as grass when used as a weapon and that the air refused me to place in it sound-waves carrying lies or insults. However, such a world would make wrong actions impossible and would render freedom of will null.

(POP, p. 382)

We need to talk about "free-will" at this point. C.S. Lewis is implying that God made man accountable for his choices. Norman Geisler explains the meaning of responsibility as "the ability or inability to respond in one way or another." CBF, p. 30, This is consistent with Genesis 2:16-17, which states that man was granted the right to eat from the tree of knowledge of good or evil. Adam was still subject to the control of God and was not granted "autonomy", which means self-law. Free-will is defined as being free from external and internal coercion but not without persuasion and influences. Man is responsible for making the decisions. God wasn't passive: He gave man both the ability to not sin and the instruction to not sin.

Geisler explains why this view of man's free will makes him responsible for his fall:

Geisler: "Adam's and Eve's free will were not the cause of their free acts; it was the power that enabled them to do so. Their actions were made possible by their will. The free agent is the efficient cause of a free action, and not their free will. The power that the free agent acts is what makes freedom possible. However, we don't say that someone is free to choose. We simply mean that they have free choice. We do the same.

It is not that man is thought, but that he has the ability to think. It is not the ability to make a choice that causes an act of freedom, but the person who holds this power. CBF Appendix 4 - the words in italics represent my addition. Underlined are words that were italicized in their original form.

Calvin is in agreement with Geisler to a certain degree:

(Calvin) I have always maintained that man was created in the

Starting, perfectly upright. (EPG, page 112) Adam fell at the behest of the Devil and his own impulse. (EPG, p. 112)

R.C. R.C:

(Sproul:) The most common definition of free-will is that it allows you to make decisions without prejudice, inclination or disposition. To be free, the will must act in a neutral position and without bias. (CBG, 51 - italics original).

It's easy to see how Calvinists and nonCalvinists can speak up for each other. Calvinists and non-Calvinists wouldn't agree with Sproul's definition of freewill. Jonathan Edwards does not have to explain how the definition is absurd to non-Calvinists. They already know it. Adam was not exempted from God's command to him not to eat from the tree containing the knowledge of good or evil. Adam gave Eve the instructions. They were also not free from being tempted by the serpent. Their will was not free from any prejudgment, inclination or disposition. Their choice was free-will. God couldn't force them to eat the forbidden fruit. Satan could not overpower Adam by forcing him to eat it. Adam and Eve had to consent to the act in order to be held accountable. They had to be able to respond in a different way to be held responsible.

Calvin acknowledges that Adam is responsible for sin. God created Adam to sin and ordained Adam to sin. This problem in Reformed Theology is called Calvinism.

Calvin: "But it couldn't be otherwise, Adam could only fall according to God's foreknowledge and will. Now, what? What then? No. He was able to fall by his full freewill and his own willful act. (EPG, p. 76)

R.C. R.C:

(Sproul) "Again, we hear the easy explanation that evil was caused by the creature's free will. It is a good thing to have free-will. God did not give us free-will. This does not mean that God is to be blamed. Man was created with the ability to sin or not sin. He chose to sin. The question is: "Why?" The question is, "Why?" This 'easy explanation' that evil was caused by Adam's free will negates the Reformed view of God directing, arranging, and dictating the fall.

R. C. Sproul continues:

(Sproul) "Herein lies your problem. A person must be able to commit an act of violence before they can do so.

To commit a sin, he must first desire to do it. Evil desires are the source of evil actions, according to the Bible. However, the mere existence of an evil desire is sin. Sin is because we are sinners. We were born with a sin nature. We are fallen beings. Adam and Eve weren't created fallen. They were free from any sin nature. They were free-willed and good creatures. They chose to sin. Why? I don't know. I have not yet found anyone who knows. (CBG, pp. 30 - 31 Note: Calvin tells us why Adam and Eve sinned. It is not the question of "why" Adam or Eve sin, but rather "how". ": Were they tempted by the willful will of God or did they do it on their own?

(Sproul) "In spite this excruciating issue we still must

Believe that God is not the author and creator of sin. The Bible doesn't answer all of our questions. However, it does reveal God's nature and character. It is impossible to imagine that God could be the creator or doer sin. (CBG, p. 31)

This is how Calvin addressed the "excruciating dilemma" of God ordaining Adam & Eve to sin & fall. It leads to the logical conclusion God is both the Author and the Doer of sin:

Calvin: "That the eternal predestination by God, which He decreed before the Fall Adam, what should happen in the entire human race and every individual within it was unalterable fixed and determined." (EPG, page 108) "Adam did not fall, nor destroy himself or his posterity without the knowledge or without the ordainingwill of God. However, this does not lessen his fault nor inflict any blame on God. (EPG, page 109 - underlined by me - original in italics)

Calvin: "Therefore, God in ordaining Fall of man, particularly, had an end most glory and most just; an ending, into which the mention or idea of sin on God's part can never enter; it is the mere thought of its entry that strikes us with horror. While I affirm that God ordered the Fall of Adam, it is not a fact that I can deny that God was the author. It is my belief, view, and sentiment that Augustine taught that God ordered the Fall of Adam. Yet, He didn't allow it to be done unwillingly. Augustine's grand and important principle cannot be denied. "That both man and apostate angels did that which God would not allow, or was contrary to HIS will; but that God's Omnipotence overrules them, that they couldn't have done it without His will." These sentiments of the holy men I agree with wholeheartedly. (EPG, p.111 underlined is mine - italics original)

Calvin: "So far, however am I not undertaking to explain this sublime hidden mystery by any powers of humans that I would ever remember, what I stated at the beginning of this discussion: That those who seek more than God has revealed to them are insane! Let us therefore delight more in wisdom than in an intoxicated and excessive curiosity to learn more about God.

permits." (EPG, pp. (EPG, pp.111-112 - italics original

Calvin: "But HOW? That God, through His foreknowledge, decree, ordained what should happen in Adam; yet, so ordained it without Him being in any way a participant of the fault or author of the transgression. How this was, I repeat is a secret that is clearly too deep to be understood by any human intellect. This is why I don't feel ashamed to admit my sins.

ignorance." (EPG, pp. (EPG, pp. 112 -113 - Italics in original – Underlined is mine. Calvin, on the other hand, asks "How?" G.K. Chesterton's quote sums it all nicely:

(Chesterton) "Only someone who knows nothing about motors speaks of

Motoring without petrol is not possible. Only a man who does not know any reason can speak of reasoning without first principles. (BC, p. 20)

This is where the difference between C. S. Lewis's first principles and Calvin's should be obvious. C. S. Lewis says that the Calvinistic view is based on a false assumption. He also believes that there is a logically contradictory view about the Omnipotence God. C. S. Lewis does not say that Calvinism is bad because it makes God the author and creator of evil. C. S. Lewis says that Calvinism is based on a logical contradiction.

This fundamental, but logically contradictory belief leads to the conclusion it must have been God's will for angels and man to fall. This belief leads us to believe that God is the Author and Motivator of evil. Calvinists' view of Omni-benevolence as God is the solution to this logical contradiction. God can sin but God doesn't want it.

=

CHAPTER FOUR

~

Calvinism's first assumption is that God can over-rule the decisions of His creatures, which could explain why God could not have stopped Adam from sin. Therefore, God must have intended for Adam to sin. We don't know what good looks like, and we can't explain why it is good for man to sin. God wills what is good. The fall took place because God wanted it to.

God can do whatever He wants. The fall must be good because God made it so. Man cannot comprehend how the fall is good. Man has such a flawed view of goodness that it appears that God ordered and allowed the fall to occur. A perfect and righteous God cannot be evil. It is obvious that God wills what He wants, and it is right because He is greater than reason.

Reformed Theology Foundation / Calvinism:

1. God can overrule the decisions of any of His creatures.

2. A. God is OmniscientB. God is OmnipotentC.

3. A. God knew that the fall would occur.

4. God could have prevented the fall from occurring.God didn't have to create anything.The fall was determined, preordained and decreed by God.

5. There is no free will in angels or men.

6. Correct because God wills it.

7. Man doesn't know what good looks like.

8. Total Depravity/Total Inability > Three meanings for Faith-------------------

A philosophical system called "voluntarism" is the answer to the problem that an Omni-benevolent God can cause evil to occur. Philosophical Voluntarism refers to the idea that God can be thought of as a form of will. It is asking the question: "Is it correct, therefore God wills?" or "Does God want something, therefore it's correct?".
Calvinism agrees to the former: God wills it, so it is right. Voluntarism is God's will. Whatever He wills, it will be right because He willed.

Martin Luther's following quote describes God as a form of will. It teaches that God wills some thing:
(Luther) "God" is the Being to whom no cause or reason can be assigned. It acts according to a standard or rule. Therefore, "What God wills is not right because He ought to or ever was bound to do so; but, on the contrary, He wills what happens because He wills." (On the Bondage and the Will, pp. 230 - 231, underline mine

Luther combines omnipotence and omniscience with voluntarism to give us the following statement:

(Luther) If we believe that God foreknows and fore-ordains everything, then He cannot be deceived or hindered in His Prescience, predestination, and will. (This is what reason herself has to admit;) so, even if reason's testimony, there can be no free-will in man, angel, or any creature. (The Bondage of the Will p. 390 underlined is mine.

These Calvin quotes show that the will is more important than reason in God's Omni-benevolence. This shows Calvin agrees with Lutheran Voluntarism:

(Calvin:) "Why does Paul specifically say that the children had not done good or evil?" However, he might get rid of all merit. Why? However, he could affirm that God used His reasons only from His own mind. (EPG, pp. 43 44 - my underline

Calvin: "Yet God had at the beginning, in His conversation to Moses, claimed to himself the free right to exercise His mercy as and towards whom He pleases. This He did so that no one could make a law about His actions. (EPG, pp. 47-48 - my underline - italics original

Calvin: "And that no law is imposed upon Him as a rule to His works: because His will can be considered better, greater, and more just than any law or rule." (EPG, p. 51. Italics in the original

Calvin: "Whenever we lift the will of God to the highest height and show that it surpasses all reason, it is impossible for us to imagine that He would ever will anything other than with the greatest reason." (EPG, p.

103 - underline is mine - italics in original)

Calvin: "It is therefore our responsibility to rest in His will alone." Our knowledge of His pleasure and will in all He does, even if it is beyond our comprehension, should suffice for us. (EPG, p.106 - italics original)

Calvin: "But what knowledge can I be said I have of the cause, if only I believe that God does what He did with a great plan and what He deemed right to do: and, especially, if all I do is pretend to be unable to understand the special and certain reason for the Divine work and counsel?" (EPG, p.106 - italics are in the original - my underline is mine).

Calvin explained that he cannot comprehend the Divine counsel and work, and then he gave the definition of Total Decavity. Man is completely incapable of understanding the things God has created.

Calvin: "What is free will?" When the Scriptures repeatedly declare that man is the slave, the prisoner, and the servant of the devil and is taken away into wickedness with all his mind and inclination, and is utterly incapable understanding or even doing the things of God? (EPG, p.192 - my underlined).

Calvinism holds that God can do whatever He wants. Nothing can happen unless God wills it. Luther's quote just explained it: All that happens is God's will. God must "ordain evil to occur" or it would not be possible. Evil exists because God has decreed or ordained it. God intended evil to occur, and God continues his will to see that it does.

Calvin agrees to Luther's assertion that all that happens is God's will:
Calvin: "Nothing is done but what the

Omnipotent could make it happen, either by allowing it to be done or by making it happen Himself. (EPG, 25 - italics original)

R.C. R.C:
(Sproul) "Then, and now, I realized that evil is a problem for me."

God's sovereignty. Is evil a result of God's sovereignty? If He did, then He is not absolute sovereign. If so, we can conclude that even evil is preordained by God in some way. (CBG, p. 29)

(Sproul) "We know God is sovereign because God is God. We must therefore conclude that God has foreordained sin. We can only conclude this conclusion. (CBG, p. 31)

Albert Mohler will show us how to see through the

Philosophical glasses of voluntarism can help you see that God allows evil to occur and is responsible for it. We are not able to understand the Divine and are therefore utterly incapable understanding His will or mind. Therefore, we don't know what good looks like. Since God's will is beyond reason, we cannot use reason to determine what "good" means for Him. ("Theodicy") is a way to reconcile God and the existence of evil. :

(Mohler) "I believe there are two additional very important issues. The whole problem with theodicy is due to a wrong question or wrong presumption. In other words, instead of seeing God as essentially goodness and deriving any good from observation of the living God, we create an abstract idea about good and then compare God against this human abstraction. This is always a loser proposition because we don't know what good looks like. That's why when people come up to us and ask if God is good, they don't realize that it is an internal contradiction. Only God exists that is good. He defines good by His consistency in his own character. He does not correspond to an arbitrary definition of what is good. This must be seen from an eschatological perspective. I believe that God will judge the ends so perfectly that the condemned will accept their right to damnation. It will be clear that evil will be shown for what it is, but God's goodness for all eternity will be revealed for all that it is. This is something we depend on our faith to see. However, we cannot fall into the trap of assuming that we are trying defend God against some human abstraction called goodness. We must simply remember that God is good and can do anything.

He is good and His will is consistent in His character. (National

Conference 2007, underlined by me

Calvinism and Voluntarism do not only argue against an "arbitrary understanding of good", but also against a "Natural Law," which allows man to determine what is good. Calvin said, "That no one might dare prescribe a law to His actions," which is exactly what a Natural Law would do. Mohler states that God is good and that whatever He does is good. God willing that evil occur is good because He will bring good from it. This is in line with Augustine and Calvin:

> (Calvin) "He also knew that it was more to His glory."

Omnipotent goodness to bring good out the evil rather than to allow evil to exist at all! (EPG, p. 25)

The Calvinist view on Omnipotence leads to the voluntarist view about the Omni-benevolence God. This teaches us that we don't know what good is. Voluntarism is the doctrine of Total Inability, Total Depravity and Total Inability. We don't know what good looks like, so we can't do it, and we cannot believe in God:

Five Points: "Because the fall, man cannot save himself by believing the gospel. The sinner is dead, blind and deaf to God's truths; his heart is corrupt and deceitful. His will is not in freedom, it is bound to his evil nature. Therefore, he cannot -- and will not - choose good over evil in this spiritual realm. It takes more than the Spirit's help to bring sinners to Christ. It takes regeneration, where the Spirit gives the sinner a new nature and makes him alive. Faith is not something that man can contribute to salvation, but it is a part God's gift for the sinner and not the sinner himself. (Five Points. p. 16 -- underlined is mine).

C. S. Lewis's statement is not supported by Calvinists:

(Lewis) "There are only two types of people in the final: those who say to God "Thy Will Be Done" and those to which God says in the final, "Thy Will be Done." (TGD, p.340 - italics original)

Calvinists would argue that C.S. Lewis's assertion is wrong, as everything that happens is God's will. God wills that the elect go up to heaven, and God wills that the reprobate go down to hell. It would be absurd to say that God does not have the final say on who goes to heaven or hell. This is because you don't "know what good is". Your sense of justice is being projected onto God. God allows evil to occur so He can bring good. "The only God that is real is a God who's good. God may allow evil to occur, but God is good and evil will still be good when we reflect on it from eternity. You don't understand why God would have you do evil, or how someone else doing it to you is evil. This is because you are "utterly incompetent of understanding the things God has done" and "don't know what goodness is." This verse, and its interpretation by Calvinists, illustrates how this belief system works:

> Joseph told them to not be afraid, for I am in the place God. You meant evil against me but God intended it for good. He wanted it to be so that many people would live as they are today.

Genesis 50:19 - 20 (ESV)

James White stated that Joseph knew exactly what his brothers were thinking when he was sold into slavery by James White. He also saw God's over-riding hand, meaning, directing and guiding him in the same act to bring about good. White also agrees that God decreed this event to take place. (PF, 48 - italics original) Reformed theology teaches that God can have a decreeing, an ordaining, a desiring, a permissive, secret, and a declaring will.

"The word that came from the LORD to Jeremiah, saying, Arise, go down to the potter's house, and I will make my words known to you there. I then went to the potter's home, and behold, he had made a work of the wheels. The vessel he had made from clay was damaged by the potter's hand, so he made another vessel. It seemed right to him to do this. Jeremiah 18 :1 - 4. (ESV – underline mine)

Calvin's commentary on Jeremiah 18. "As clay is subject to the will and power of the potter so are men: God is then compared with the potter. "God decided, before the creation, how he felt about each person."

Calvinism holds that God intended for the fall to occur. God wanted Adam to sin and be marred in order that God could make Adam and all of Adam's descendants into whatever He pleases. God intentionally marred the clay vessel that was in His hand so that He could make it again as He pleases. Adam didn't harm himself against the Omnipotent will overruling God. Adam marred himself according to the permissive will and the Omnipotent will of God. This is a long quote from Calvin that explains that Jeremiah 18 vessels were made in this way by God and not through their own actions:

(Calvin:) "Now, if this being "afore ready unto glory" was a peculiar and particular to the elect, it seems that the rest of the non-elect were also "fitted to destroy:" because they had already been devoted to certain destruction by their nature. It is absurd to think that they were "fitted for destruction" by their wickedness. True, the reprobate are the ones who bring on their own the wrath and they constantly seek to have it fall upon themselves. It must be admitted that the apostle refers to the difference between the elect (and the reprobate) that results from God's only secret will and purpose. (EPG, p. 60)

After we have reviewed the Calvinist position, let me review how C. S. Lewis got to the same point. He also has a different view about the Omnibenevolence God. C. S. Lewis's first assumption is that God cannot have prevented Lucifer or man from sin. God intended Lucifer and Man to have free-will. However, they used it against His will. It is also logically inconsistent to claim that God can simultaneously give man free will and withhold it. --------------------

Foundation of Classical Theism:
1. God can give His creatures freedom at will.
2. A. God is OmniscientB. God is Omnipotent
    C.   God is Perfect

3. A. God knew that the fall would occur.

4. The fall could not be stopped by God. God didn't have to create anything. The fall wasn't ordained by God. God gave man the power to choose.

5. Angels and man are "Free Moral Agents".

6. God knows what is right. (Man was created so God could Love us.

7. Man's ability to discern good from evil is affected.

8.   Unrighteous with impaired abilities > Faith - ability believe - common for all.--------------------

C.   S. Lewis discusses whether we can determine what good is:(Lewis) "Any consideration at all of the goodness God"

The following dilemma threatens us.

One, God can be wiser than us.

Our views may differ from yours in many areas, not only on good and bad. Therefore, what may seem to us to be good may not be good to Him. And what may appear to us to be evil may not be bad to Him.

However, God may have a different moral judgment than we do, so our 'black' might be His white'. We cannot call Him good if we say that God is good, but claim that His goodness is completely different from ours. A completely unknown quality in God is not moral grounds for us to love or obey Him. If God is not in our sense 'good,' we will obey Him, if at any point, through fear, and should equally be ready to obey an all-powerful Fiend. The doctrine of Total Depravity, which states that our notion of good is not worth anything because we are completely depraved, may turn Christianity into devil-worship. (POP, 384 -- underline mine).

C. S. Lewis explains why we don't always know what good looks like. Our ability to recognize what good is is impaired:

(Lewis) "The Divine goodness' differs slightly from ours but it isn't totally different. It differs not as white or black, but as a perfect circular form from a child's first attempt at drawing a wheel. However, once the child learns to draw, the circle it makes will be what it is.

 "I was trying to make it from the beginning."

(Lewis) "This doctrine has been presupposed by Scripture. Christ calls on men to repentance -- a call that would be meaningless if God's standards were completely different from what they had already practiced and knew. He appeals to our moral judgment -- "Why even of yourself judge yet what is right?" (Luke 12 :57) God expostulates with men in the Old Testament on the basis their conceptions of gratitude and fidelity; and places Himself before His creatures - 'What iniquity has your fathers found in Me, that they have gone far from me' " (Jeremiah 2:15) (POP p. 385: Acts 17:30: Call to repent).

C. S. Lewis explains how he believes that something is good and God will grant it. There is an inherent right and wrong or natural law. He also points out that voluntarism is a logical conclusion:

(Lewis) "Sometimes it has been asked if God commands certain things simply because they are right or if certain things are right because God commands them. The first option is the one I strongly support. Hooker and Dr Johnson are both against me. The second could lead to the terrible conclusion (reported, I think by Paley), that charity is only good because God has ordered it. That He could equally have ordered us to hate Him and each other would have been correct. Contrary to popular belief, I think they err if they believe that God will do this or that He has other reasons. (Hooker Laws of Eccl. Polity, I, I, 5.) God's wisdom, which sees and is always good, determines His will. His goodness embraces the intrinsically good. (POP, p. 409)

C. S. Lewis and Calvin both have to answer the following question: Is there a correct way of doing things, so God wills them? Or: Does God will it be correct? Calvin chooses voluntarism, and C. S. Lewis takes the second option. C. S. Lewis chooses the first option, which is known as "intellectualism". It is easy to determine if voluntarism really is true by comparing its logical conclusion with scripture. Albert Mohler said, "We don't know what good looks like." God the Father has some words to share about this:

"The LORD God then said, "Behold, this man is now like one of us in knowing good and bad." He should not reach out and grab the tree of life, eat, and live forever. Therefore, the LORD God sent him from the garden to make the ground. Genesis 3:22-23 (ESV – Underlined is mine).

Scripture tells us that God has made us like Him in our ability of knowing good from bad.

Calvin says that man is completely incapable of understanding God's things.

Mohler says that man doesn't know what good looks like.

Scripture teaches us that God and man can know the difference between good and bad.

We can agree with Calvin and Mohler about the fact that man doesn't know what goodness is and Scripture says that God and man have similar abilities to know what goodness is. The absurd conclusion is that neither man nor God know what good looks like.

It is easy to see that Reformed Theology, voluntarism and Scripture are both in error by simply comparing them.

Intellectualism is a belief that there is an intrinsic good or evil, which is contrary to voluntarism. There is a reason God does what He wills. Love, for example, is intrinsically good because it carries its goodness within:

"Love is kind, patient, and kind; it doesn't envy or boast; It is not."

Arrogant and rude It doesn't insist on its way. Love endures all things. It believes all things and bears all burdens. Love never ends. Prophecies will end, just like tongues and knowledge. 1 Corinthians 13:4-8 (ESV).

As Love is intrinsically good and sin intrinsically bad, so is Sin: "For you aren't a God who enjoys in wickedness; evil might not be your favorite."

You are my companion. You will not allow the boastful to stand before you; you will hate all evildoers. Psalms 5 - 4 (ESV).

Hate is not the same as sin or evil. I will hate someone simply because they are their skin color. If I hate evil I do good.

"Seek goodness and not evil so that you can live; and so, the LORD.

As you have stated, the God of Hosts will be with your. Love good and hate evil and bring justice to the gate. It is possible that the LORD, God of Hosts, will be kind to the remaining Joseph. Amos 5:14-15 (ESV). Remember Chapter Two's quote: "This doesn't make God submissive to anything beyond Himself." God is only subject to logic (good reason) when He is also subject to his own nature as He is the ultimate Reason (John 1:1). The law of justice is the same. God is not bound to anything outside Himself. He is only bound to His unchangeable nature. (ST 1, p. 91)

(Lewis)

Value is the belief that some attitudes are true and others are false. It refers to the nature of the universe and the kinds of things we are. (Abolition, page 473 - words in brackets are mine).

G.K. Chesterton also describes the intrinsically good:
(Chesterton) "Reason, justice grip the farthest and the most remote places."

The lonely star. Take a look at these stars. They look like single sapphires and single diamonds. You can think of any crazy botany or geology. Imagine a forest of adamants with brilliant leaves. Imagine the moon as a single blue sapphire, or as a single elephantine. Don't think that all that frantic, chaotic astronomy would make any difference to the reason or justice of conduct. You would still find a noticeboard saying "Thou shalt never steal" on plains of opal under cliffs made of pearl. (BC, p. 29).

Our ability to recognize good instead of being unable to determine what it is has been diminished. As Lucifer's judgment became impaired by pride, Adam's was also affected by the temptation of the serpent.

Geisler explains why we don't know exactly what good looks like:
Geisler: "Another clue to understanding natural revelation are our basic moral inclinations. Our best understanding of natural law is not based on our actions, but our reactions to them. We are able to see the moral law intuitively. It doesn't matter if we read it in a book. We can intuitively know the moral law, as written by our hearts. When interpreting natural law, it is important to interpret it from true reactions. These are not always the actions we do to others but more often the ones that we want to see done to us. Paul again relates to this point when Paul writes about the "things we do by nature" that "show the moral law "written upon our hearts" (Romans 2:14 - 15).

Geisler: "Our moral inclinations can be seen in how we react when others violate our rights. We don't see the moral laws nearly as clearly when other people violate our rights. Herein is revealed our depravity. Our sinfulness does not lie in our inability or unwillingness to fulfill our moral duties to others.

Geisler: "The type of reactions that demonstrate the natural moral law were forcefully brought home to me as a professor after carefully

After reading a well-researched student paper on moral relativity, I wrote "F. I don't like blue folders." The student protested after he was given his grade and stormed into the office of his professor. It's not fair! This is not just! His true measure of morality was not what he wrote on paper, but what God had written inside him. When he was wronged, he saw the truth of what he believed to be right. (ST 1, pp.

75-76 - italics original

On page 14 of Chosen By God, R. C. Sproul lists Saint Thomas Aquinas teaching the "Reformed view". Aquinas formulated Classical Theism. This belief holds that God is infinitely simple in His essence, while His creatures are complex. Sproul uses Classical Theism as a way to explain how God's attribute Love and God's attribute Of Sovereignty relate to each other: (Sproul) "When we think of love as an attribute, we see that it is defined in relation all the other attributes. This holds true for love as well as all other attributes of God. When we refer to the attributes of God, it is important to keep in mind that these properties cannot be reduced to their individual parts. We affirm that God is not a complex being. We confess that God is a simple entity. This doesn't mean God is easy. Simplicity is not equated with difficulty, but with composition. Composite beings are made up of specific parts. A human being is a composite.

I'm made up of many parts: arms, legs and eyes.

(Sproul) "As a simple entity, God isn't made up of the same parts as us. This is essential to understanding the nature of God. This is because God is not partially immutable, partially omniscient, partly omnipotent or partly infinite. He is not made up of a single section of being. God is not merely a collection of attributes, but He is the sum total of His attributes. This means that all attributes of God help to define His other attributes in simple terms, as opposed to more complicated terms. When we say God is immutable we also mean that His immutability includes an eternal immutability and omnipotent immutability as well as a holy immutability and a loving immutability. The same goes for His love. It is immutable, eternal, omnipotent, holy, and a holy love. (Loved, pp. 6 - 7 – underlined is mine - italics original

To this point, Sproul accurately represents what Aquinas outlined in his Summa Theologica. This philosophical system is known as "Classical Theism". It states, in its simplest form, that God is "absolutely simple" (meaning "indivisible") while all the creatures He created are "composed" (meaning they have "potentiality," or the ability to change or be changed).

A simple God can't change. He is "immutable". God is already perfect and cannot be made more perfect. God is omniscient and cannot be more aware. God's attributes are "extensive," meaning that each attribute can be extended to all other attributes. God is able and able to love perfectly. This is the same sentence, with each attribute in parentheses. God (Omniscience), knows how to love (Love) perfectly and is able to do so (Omnipotence). His love is immutable (unchangeable). This view of God is shared by C. S. Lewis, Sproul, Aquinas and Sproul.

God is different from His creation, which has potentiality. The tree can grow and change. A tree can be chopped down and turned into a table. This book changed my life. You've grown up and have learned something. One third of angels and Lucifer's fall taught the angels. This distinction shows how important it is to define the attributes of God.

R. C. Sproul continues and explains why Calvinists view sovereignty as an attribute of God, which is part of the simple, indivisible essence of God:

When I'm lecturing about the holiness and sovereignty of God, justice of God or the wrath, it is often interrupted by someone who says, "But my God...a God of love." I quickly assure the person that I believe in a God who loves. However, I am often struck by the suggestion in the protest that God's love is somehow incompatible or incompatible with His holiness, justice and sovereignty, or his wrath. The attribute of love is now isolated from all other attributes of God so that it is either the only attribute God knows or subsumes or swallows all His attributes.

This is exactly what happens when God is conceived as a combination of many different beings. This structure allows us to choose the attributes we want and gives us the freedom to create a god that is idol-like. If the Bible is our main source of God's revelations about His nature and character, it states that God is holy and just, sovereign and wrathful as well as loving. We need to understand God's love in such a manner that it doesn't negate or swallow these other attributes.

 (Loved, pp. 8-9 - my underline

(Sproul: This reveals that God's sovereignty is behind or alongside His electing love. This reveals that God's will is sovereign, but that His love is sovereign as well. (Loved, p.89 - my underline)

It is easy to conclude that God is sovereign over His Love. This explains why God could Love Jacob but Hate Esau even before the twins did anything good or bad. Aquinas agrees with Sproul that "Love" is an attribute God. Sproul agrees with Aquinas that God is sovereign. The difference between Classical Theists and Calvinists is the way God is sovereign:

The following explanation comes from Geisler's Systematic Theology. It will explain how these views differ from one another:

Geisler: "How many attributes do God have?"?

Different theologians may list different numbers. The reason is that not all theologians have a complete list. (2) Some theologians combine different attributes into one. (3) Partly because there is disagreement about whether certain attributes are attributes or activities of God (e.g. Mercy; and (4) because some theologians don't distinguish between an attribute, which is part of God's essence such as holiness, and a characteristic, which is something that is just something that belongs God in general such as ineffability.

God also has other non-moral characteristics

These are God's essential attributes and how He relates to His creatures. These include sovereignty, transcendence and immanence as well as omnipresence, omnipresence and ineffability. God wouldn't be sovereign over, transcendent above or immanent in a creation without it.

God's essential attributes are, however, inherent to His nature as such. (ST 2, p. 20-21 underlined is mine)

R. C. Sproul says that God is both sovereign and loving, which implies that they can be combined. God will be lovingly sovereign and God is sovereign over his love.

Geisler says that God's attribute love is not essential and sovereignty does not extend to God's attributes of love. The essence of God gives rise to sovereignty: God is sovereign because He's all-powerful, all good, all-knowing and all-wise. Classical Theists agree that God can do whatever He wants, but it is His nature to be sovereign in a manner that is compatible with

His nature. Classical Theists are in agreement with Calvinists about the supremacy of Nature over man's will. Classical Theists believe that God's Nature is superior to God's Will, and that God's will flows from His essence or nature.

God cannot allow that evil to happen, since God is Light. (1 John 1:5)

Voluntarism, contrary to Classical Theism teaches that God can be seen as a form of will. This view could place God's will above God's nature, or make God's will identical with God's nature (instead the nature being superior to God's will, or God's will flowing from His essence or nature).

Summa Theologica states that Aquinas includes "providence" as a part of God's essence. Providence is God's means of controlling all things, while sovereignty is God's right to do so. The means God has in control is Providence. It is His attributes Omnipotence and Omnibenevolence, Omniscience and Wisdom. These attributes are inherent in God's nature and reflect His essence. God is sovereign because He has the right of using these attributes. Sovereignty is one of God's essential attributes. It is an attribute that He attributes to Himself, but it is not an attribute in itself. This misunderstanding by Sproul may be the reason he incorrectly labels Aquinas Reformed.

All Calvinists are driven to a Voluntaristic view on the Omnipotence and Benevolence of God by the reformed view in relation to the Fall. John Duns Scotus agrees with Reformed theology on the attribute of

Omnipotence. Scotus taught that God's attributes should be understood unambiguously, which leads to the reformation of Omnibenevolence as Voluntaristic.

C. S. Lewis' view on the Omnipotence God in relation to the Fall, ends in the philosophy Intellectualism. Aquinas and the Classical Theists agree that Omnipotence must be understood analogically. This leads to the Classical

Toist's view on intellectualism in relation to the Omni-benevolence God. After Aquinas, this view of Omnipotence is called "Thomism".

There is another curious result from the reformed view that God is sovereign over His Love. In their struggle to find an alternative to Calvinism, some Arminians have used the same reasoning as Calvinists but with different attributes. When sovereignty is in the essence of God as Calvinists contend, sovereignty extends to every other attribute of God, not just to Love. Just as Calvinists have what are called "hyper-Calvinists", Arminians have what are called "Open Theists". This view joins sovereignty with Omniscience just as Calvinists join sovereignty with Love. Just as God is sovereign over His love in Calvinism: choosing to love some and choosing to hate others for no other reason than that He wills it, Open Theists believe that God is sovereign over His Omniscience: choosing to know some things, and choosing to not know other things. In effect, saying that God chooses to not know everything that will happen so that He can derive pleasure from being surprised at what happens (I hope this is a fair portrayal of Open Theism). The only point I am trying to make is that the modification of Classical Theism that is made by Calvinists ends up leaving them defenseless against a view that they believe is heresy.

The best argument to counter Classical Theism or "Divine Essentialism", is to argue that sovereignty is essential to God's nature, since God the Father is sovereign above the Son and Spirit. This reasoning introduces a hierarchy to the divine essence, and is called the heresy or subordinationism by both Calvinists as well as Classical theists.

Norman Geisler explains Subordinationism:

Geisler: "This heresy was held Justin Martyr, Origen, and condemned by the Council of Constantinople (381). It states that the Son is subordinate to the Father in nature. Subordinationism should not be confused with the orthodox belief in which the Son (Christ), is functionally subordinated to (i.e. Subordinationism is not to be confused with the orthodox belief that the Son (Christ) is functionally subordinate to (i.e.,. (ST 2, p. 297

Original text in italics and parentheses

C. S. Lewis' view of Classical Theism will be the focus of this discussion. Classical Theists believe sovereignty is a characteristic that God possesses and that He attributes to it. Because God created nothing that He could be sovereign over, sovereignty is not necessary to God's nature. Providence is the way God is sovereign. Omniscience, Omnipresence and Omnipotence are all examples of this. God is sovereign because He is who He is. Therefore, sovereignty flows from His nature. However, it is not essential to His Nature and does not cover the attributes essential to His nature. While love is at the core of God's essence, sovereignty is not. Classical Theists don't believe God has sovereignty over His love like Calvinists.

The following illustration has been very helpful in my discussions about the relationship between God's attributes. Imagine a bowl empty sitting on a table. You place a cherry in the bowl for each attribute you name. Omnipotence, Omniscience,

Perfection, Wisdom, Light, etc. Calvinists would name Sovereignty and Transcendence, Immanence and Omnipresence as attributes of God and then place a cherry in each bowl. These descriptions of God would be considered attributes by a classical theist.

Classic theists would not place a cherry in each bowl. The Omnipotence cherry would go in a bowl and the Sovereignty would be on the table beside the bowl. God is known for His attributes such as Sovereignty and Transcendence, Omnipresence (Immanence), Omnipresence (Immanence), and Ineffability. God is sovereign because He is Omnipotent and Omni-benevolent. He is also Omniscient.

Another example is to look at the relationship between your breathing and your lungs. When you take a deep breath, you say you are actually breathing. You would not say that you are "lunging" if I looked at you. It is because you have lungs, that you breathe. The same is true for the relationship between Grace and Love. Scripture says that God is Love. In my illustration, the Grace of God is derived from the Love of God (represented by the lungs). God is Love (Lungs) and He is gracious (breathing). Romans 5:8 states, "God showed his love for us by sending Christ to die for us while we were still sinners." (ESV). I wouldn't say "God is Grace" any more than I would say you are my lungs when you breathe. I would instead say that God is gracious, and that you are breathing. Also, I would add that Christ died because God is Love. Just as I would say that you can breathe because you have lungs.

The Natural Law is also supported by Classical Theists. Calvin's objection to Intellectualism or a Natural Law is that it prescribes laws for God's actions: Calvin: "And He did this, so that no one might dare prescribe a law to His actions." (EPG, p. 47)

Augustine and Calvin both agree that the first principle of Calvinism is that God must have the power to overrule all of His creatures' decisions. God is neither Omnipotent nor Sovereign. This rule establishes a law that governs the actions of God. An Omnipotent God must have the ability to overrule the decisions of His creatures. God therefore has no obligation to give any freedom to His creatures. Reformed Theology's initial point prescribes a law to govern God's actions, which is exactly what Calvin taught should not be done.

Another reason why Sproul shouldn't have listed Aquinas is because

Reformed since Aquinas also advocated for a Natural Law. C. S. Lewis points out in The Abolition of Man that those who are not subject to the Natural law do not have any grounds for criticizing the Natural law. (Abolition, p. 481) C. S. Lewis spends Book One in Mere Christianity explaining how the Natural Law "is the foundation of all clear thinking about us and the universe in which we live". (MC, p. 13)

The first principle of Classical Theism states that God can give freedom to His creations. No matter what theological system you choose to follow, you will end up following a set or laws for God's actions.

=

Chapter Five

~

In the last few chapters, I tried to follow Abraham.

Joshua Heschels advice to "present the perspective where the original understanding was made". We can understand the perspectives from which the views of the freedom and power of God, as well as the Omnibenevolence and Omnipotence, were developed. This will help us understand the differences between the views on the Sovereignty and fall of man and angels.

Before I explain how these foundational beliefs can lead to two distinct systematic theologies, I want to briefly examine a few concepts:

First, I will explain why bad things happen for good people. This explanation is what I call the "tapestry argument".

Tapestry argument is a popular explanation for why evil exists or why bad things happen to good people. It looks something like this:

~

God weaves a beautiful tapestry every day. Sometimes God allows or wills evil to occur. When this happens, it is reflected in the tapestry as a dark spot. This dark spot is all that we see when we look up at the tapestry. The tapestry God is weaving is beautiful when we look back at it.

~

Most of us are familiar with the comforting phrase that "everything happens because of a reason ...""". I've heard many stories about how God brought on great personal loss that led to redemption and brought a person to Christ.

It is easy to imagine that, without the adversity and evil in their lives, they wouldn't have felt the need for help or turned to Christ for salvation.

For the tapestry argument, the most popular example is the work on the cross. God chose the worst evil, the death of His Son, in order to bring salvation.

It is important to remember that evil exists because God has a purpose. Evil exists because God has a purpose.

It is okay that evil exists. God wants evil to occur so He can bring good.

This illustration was probably created around 100 years after Calvin and Gottfried Leibniz, who were both philosophers who wrote Theodicy. His book focuses on the fact that this world is the best that God could have made. This is the most perfect world God could have made, and it is full of evil. The world God created is the most perfect, and it has no evil.

The tapestry argument is described by Leibniz in On the Ultimate Origin of Things. The evils God wants to see are the confused colors or thoughtless smears. These can be seen from afar and transform into works of art:

~

(Leibniz) "Let's look at a beautiful picture and cover it so that we can only see a small portion of it. What else will be in it? No matter how closely we examine it or how close we approach it, other than a confused mass of colors and no art. But if we take off the covering and look at it from the right perspective, we'll see that the artist of the work has executed what looked like haphazardly on the canvas with the highest art.

~

      Also, see On the Radical Origination Of Things:

~

(Leibniz) "If we take a beautiful picture and cover it only in a small spot, what will be there? It doesn't matter how much we study it. Instead of a confusing mixture of colors that lack beauty or art, it becomes a very beautiful picture." When the cover is removed, and the entire painting is viewed in a way that suits it best, we discover that what appeared to be a smear on the canvas was actually a work of art by the artist.

~

     Any evil that has occurred is called the "thoughtless smear" of the artist. This could include the crucifixion or the holocaust.

     Although Leibniz may be the original creator of the tapestry illustration but Augustine laid the foundations for theological theology:

~

(Calvin/Augustine:) "That God the Lord of All Things, who created everything'very good', foreknew that evil would arise from this good. And He also knew that it was more to His glory to bring good out evil than to allow evil to exist at all! (EPG, p. 25)

~

These four points can be derived from the Augustine quote:
   1. God allowed evil to exist through His permissive will.
2.   God created evil in order to bring good out of it. God makes good of evil in order to give glory to Hisself.4. Conclusion: God allows evil to occur, but He can make good of it and bring glory to Himself.

~

The R. C. Spul quote in chapter 3 gives a great example of the tapestry argument:

~

(Sproul) "Evil is when it comes into the world through God's design, and God's sovereign will. It is a crime to call evil good or evil evil. But God orders it to occur and God is all good. He only ordains what is good. It is bad that evil exists, but God would not allow it to be. This isn't too difficult.

~

These four points are based on the quote above:

1. God sovereignly wills that evil enters the world.
2. It is a crime to call evil good.
3. If God wills or orders it, evil is allowed to occur.
4.   Only God can give good things.~

These four points can be summed up as follows:

1. Because God created evil, it is good.
2. All that God wills, is good.
3. God allows evil to occur so that He can make good.
4.   God wills good and God wills evil. Therefore, evil is good.~

The tapestry argument concludes that evil is good. Sproul said that it was a sin to label evil good, and Calvin says that sin is contrary to God's nature. (EPG, p.

187)

In the two previous chapters, we have examined the fall and concluded that God didn't allow or will permit it to occur. This view is consistent in Scripture and avoids the errors of "tapestry arguments", which end with the conclusion evil is good.

The crucifixion is used as a "tapestry argument" to show that God intended evil to occur so He could make good of it and bring glory to Himself. This leads to the conclusion, that Jesus died for our sins by being crucified.

Scripture says that the greatest form of love is to give your life for your friend (John 15 13). Christ did not sacrifice His life to save us. This good, the atonement for sins, is what God intended should occur.

God intended that Adam and Eve would have free-will. God also wanted His Son to do the same by giving His life in order to buy us the precious blood of His Son.

The evil of the Crucifixion was not planned by God. God wanted His only begotten Son to atone for our sins. Although the act of crucifixion of sinners was evil and God didn't allow it to occur, He did not "permit" the evil of the Crucifixion. God instead commanded that His Son should atone for our sins. The atonement was not just good. God intended for the glorious and great atonement.

Satan intended for the evil of the Crucifixion. God could not allow Jesus to become sin for us. Habakkuk 1:13 says that God had to turn his back on Christ. "His eyes were too pure to see evil." Satan was the one who chose to try to destroy Jesus.

The Wardrobe, The Lion, The Witch, and the Wardrobe, reveals that Edmund's family betrayed him by allowing the witch to claim the rights to Edmund. Aslan couldn't just give in to the witch and eat her head off, freeing Edmund. Aslan had to give himself to the witch to save Edmund. Aslan was killed by the witch.

Voluntarism is the belief that God has a permissive mind, which allows evil to occur. We see God through the "glasses" of voluntarism. He uses His permissive will for evil to occur. We attribute blessings to God when we experience good things. Voluntarism, then, divides God into many separate wills. Augustine and Sproul, however, will agree with Lewis and Aquinas that God is indivisible (absolutely simple) in His essence.

Voluntarism, as we have seen in the preceding chapter, is the belief that God can be understood as a form of will. God can have a prescriptive, desiring, ordaining, secret, permissive, and/or decreeing will. This view of God leads to God being divided into many wills.

It's easier to grasp the idea of God being conceived as some kind of will when I compare it to the opposite viewpoint of God being conceived as His attributes. His attributes make up His essence, which is superior to His will. His will flows from His nature. We can only understand God's essence as a simple one and the attributes that make it up, which allows us to see that only one will flow from that essence.

Instead of thinking of God only as a type of will, consider God to be Omnipotent, Omnibenevolent Wise, Love and Omnipotent. This view shows that evil was created against God's will. A God who cannot do something is greater than one that can. A God that cannot make nonsense is larger than one that can. A God who cannot lie is greater than one that can lie. A God that cannot forgive sins unless justice is served is greater than one that can forgive sins with no atonement. He simply crucifies His Son to bring joy to Himself. This is the danger of believing in 'absolute sovereignty'. If God were absolutely sovereign, He could have forgiven Lucifer, and all mankind, rendering the crucifixion unnecessary.

The Tapestry Argument, which states that evil is good because God wills it to happen in order to bring glory to Hisself, leads to the conclusion evil is good. We all would agree that it is wrong to call evil good. We all agree it is a sin that evil is called good. Therefore, it is wrong to claim that God wills evil to occur by His permissive will, His ordainingwill, secret will or any other will.

The next chapter focuses on the contrast between the systematic theologies of Calvin, C. S. Lewis, and the following chapter.

=

CHAPTER SIX

~

"Whatever the LORD wills, He does in heaven as well as on earth.

In the seas and deeps." Psalms 135 :6 (ESV).

&

"Have you any pleasure in the death the wicked, declares God

GOD and not that he should live in obedience to his will? Ezekiel

18:23 (ESV)

&

"First, let me urge you to make intercessions, prayers and supplications.

Let us give thanks to all people, kings, and those in high places, so that we can live a quiet, peaceful, godly, and dignified life. This is good and pleasing to God our Savior. He desires that all people be saved and come to the truth. There is only one God and one mediator between Gods and men: the man Christ Jesus who offered himself as a ransom for all. This testimony was given at the right time. 1 Timothy 2:1 - 6 (ESV)

Because God is able to do anything He wants, and He desires that all people be saved, the obvious conclusion from these verses can be universalism. However, Calvin and C. S. Lewis both believe that not all men will be saved. Each person takes a different approach because of how they came to this conclusion.

Calvinism holds that an Omnipotent God can save all men. This means that God must will that some men go into hell. It is hard to imagine how this could be beneficial. However, since the only God who exists is an all-good God we cannot know what good is. We are completely depraved, and we lack the ability to seek God because we don't know what good looks like. We don't know what good is in man and cannot understand why God would condemn them to hell. Therefore, we can't believe that certain men will be saved by God because of their actions. Both the Voluntaristic view and Unconditional election lead to the conclusion of God's preordained creation and destiny for man. The logical progression of the system, which is built on Augustine's faith foundation, is so evident that you can see that Calvin believed it and taught it.

Reformed Theology Foundation / Calvinism:
1.   God can overrule the decisions of any of His creatures.

    2.   A. God is OmniscientB. God is OmnipotentC.

3.   A. God knew that the fall would occur.

4.   God could have prevented the fall from occurring.God didn't have to create anything.The fall was planned, preordained and decreed by God.

5.   There is no free will in angels or men.

6.   It is God's will that it be done. > Created for God's Glory.

7.   Man doesn't know what good looks like.

8.   Total Depravity, Total Inability. > Three definitions of faith.

9.   Unconditional election. > Predetermination independent ofForeknowledge.

10.   Limited Atonement. > God able to save all - will save all that Jesus diedfor.

11.   Irresistible Effectual Grace > Grace universal

12.	The perseverance of the Saints. > Those who "fall from faith" are never saved.-------------------

R. C. Sproul: "First, we must ask the question: "Does God have power to save everyone?" It is certain that God has the power to change the hearts of all impenitent sinners and bring them to Him. He cannot have such power if He does not possess it. Why doesn't He use that power for all? (CBG, p. 35; my underlined is mine).

Dr. Jonathan Gerstner says: "We pray through the work of Spirit, readers at The Potter's Freedom and Dr. Geisler will see the truth about the only true God who is sovereign over all matters, including the salvation or damnation of man." (PF, p. 38 - my underlined text

Calvin taught that God can give faith to everyone and has the power of saving all:

Calvin: "Where God is unwilling to bestow the gift or to show mercy, it is a display His truth that declares that no one can come to Christ to whom He has not given the will. They are not drawn by Him, even though He is able to do so. (EPG, p.87 underlined is mine).

(Calvin) "Christ also here proclaims, through this His doctrine that those who are effectually drawn toward Him whose minds or hearts God "compels", are effective." (EPG, 34 - my underline)

Calvinists believe that an Omnipotent God can make or compel any sinner to choose Him. But God doesn't choose to do this. Jesus Christ would have died for everyone if God wanted all to be saved. God cannot want all saved, since not all will be saved. This would indicate that God is not Omnipotent. In his response to Georgius, Calvin challenges God's desire to save all:

"But Paul teaches us (continues Georgius), that God 'would like all men to be saved. According to his interpretation of the passage, it follows that either

God has failed in His plans or all men must be saved. If he replies that God wants all men to be saved on His part or as far as He cares, then he will see.

However, salvation is left up to each individual's free will. I ask him in return why God didn't command that the Gospel be preached to everyone, regardless of their background, right from the beginning. Why did He allow so many generations to wander in the darkness of death for so many years? In the context of the apostle, it is clear that God "would have all people come to the knowledge the truth." The meaning of the entire passage is clear and straightforward. It contains no ambiguity for any reader of candour or sound judgment. In the previous pages, we have explained the entire passage. The apostle had previously exhorted that solemn and general prayers be offered up in Church "for kings" etc. so that no one could have cause to be deplored those kings or magistrates whom God might be pleased with setting over them. Because rulers were at that time the most violent enemies to the faith. Paul makes Divine provision for this situation by praying to the Church and affirming that Christ's grace could reach this order of men, including rulers, princes, and kings of all descriptions. (EPG, pp. (EPG, pp.151-152 - parentheses and italics in the original)

Because God doesn't want all saved, Jesus didn't give His life as a ransom:
(Calvin) "John extends the benefits of atonement to

Christ, who was complete by His death, is available to all elect of God in any climes throughout the world. However, this does not change the fact that the reprobate live in harmony with the elect throughout the world. (EPG, p. 150. Italics in the original

Calvin says that Jesus died only for the elect, wherever they may be in the world. Jesus didn't die for the reprobate who are mixed in with the elect.

(Calvin) "Be it noted, however, when I refer to reconciliation through Christ being offered unto all, I don't mean that the message or embassy by which

Paul claims God "reconciles all the world unto Himself" really arrives or reaches all men. But that it is not sealed randomly on all who receive it, so that they are effective in it. Our opponent is arguing that there is "no acceptance of people with God." He must first "go learn" what "person" means, according to our explanations. Then we will have no trouble with him on this point. (EPG, p. 151)

James White explains why Calvin said that:

(White: The prescriptive will and law of God, which... calls all men to repent, and gives the gift of repentance to the elect in the regeneration, is It doesn't follow that God will not call the elect to repentance if the law doesn't command it.

everyone." (PF, p.149-150 - italics original)

(White:) "We don't here refer to God's revealed will found."

In His law, which commands all men to repent, we speak of His saving will for all elect to repent and His ability to do that will. (PF, p. 151)

The scriptures support the belief that God requires repentance from everyone:
"The times of ignorance God ignored, but He now commands

All people worldwide must repent." Acts 17:30 (ESV).

Calvin: "For when God exhorts people to repent and then offers them life upon their return, that exhortation is common to all men. God gives His children the unimaginable privilege of taking their "stony hearts" and giving them "hearts made of flesh." (EPG, p. 157)

Calvin says that Christ's atoning work is available to all people, but that it was intended to only save those who Christ had sacrificed:
"All who Christ has sacrificed Hisself for will be saved

infallibly." (Five Points, p. 39)

"Christ" (Christ) "came into this world to save and represent those who were given to Him by God." Christ's saving work was therefore limited in that it was intended to save a few, but not in its value. If God had intended it, it would have guaranteed salvation for all. (Five Points p. 39, words in parentheses my addition).

Calvin: "Now we won't allow the common solution to this question to apply on the current occasion. That would have it Christ suffered enough for all men but only for His elect. This absurdity, through which our monk gained so much praise amongst his fraternity, is of no consequence to me."

(EPG, p. 150)

It is being asked: For whom did Jesus die? Are the elect only eligible for the atonement or are they all? Both sides agree that His sacrifice is sufficient for all men. Both sides agree that the atonement works for all elect. Calvin considers this statement absurd because it does not answer the question of Jesus' purpose. He believes that the reprobate are exempted from the atonement.

Calvinists can offer at least two reasons for the fact that God doesn't want everyone to be saved. He never intended to save everybody. First, voluntarism. This is when God asks why some people will be saved while others will be condemned. It is to respond against God and argue that God's justice is measured by human justice. (see EPG, page 116) The second reason God created angels and men is to bring glory to Himself:

Calvin: "The Lord has as a motive for all His works His own great glory. This is His ultimate goal in all of them. (EPG, p.105 - italics original)

(Calvin) "The reprobate have been set apart in the purpose God for to the end, so that God might demonstrate His power in them." (EPG, p. 50)

Calvin: "Therefore, we do not imply absurdity when we declare that God created the race of man for His glory, even though He did not need anything to add to Himself." This should be considered, most deservedly, the greatest and most essential end of man's existence. (EPG, p. 68)

(Calvin: "... "The wicked were made for evil," only because God wanted to reveal His glory in them. (EPG, p.

69)

Calvin: "What is the future of all the Scripture testimonies that declare the glory of God the ultimate goal and highest object of salvation?" Let us therefore hold on to this wonderful truth: God's mind in salvation was not to forget Him, but to place His glory first and foremost; and that He created the entire world for His glory, so that it could be a magnificent stage whereon He can shine His glory. (EPG, p. 69)

John Piper discusses the primacy and voluntarism of God's will, and agrees with Calvin about the glory of God:

(Piper) "It is the glory and essence of God to give mercy (but also wrath Exodus 34.7) to whomever He chooses, without any restriction imposed by anyone other than His will. This is what God is all about. This is His name. (The Justification of God Piper, John. pp. 88-89 - parentheses are in the original, underline mine

(Piper) "The chief goal of God is to glorify God, enjoy Him forever. God is able to do anything He pleases.

Him happy." (Desiring God, Piper, John. Ch. 1)

(R.C. (R.C. (CBG, p. 24)

(White:) Predestination is founded upon the divine purpose and nothing else. This purpose comes from the Sovereign, who "works all things according to His will." This is the Christian confession. God is sovereign over all. It is clear that salvation for human beings is within the realm God's control. (PF, p. 181 Italics in Original - Quote Marks in Original)

White: "God works all things according to His will. This includes His predestination of men and women for salvation. The (Ephesians 1:22) result is a repetition of a fundamental truth: salvation is for the glory of God. A biblical teaching does not include any teaching that is in any way detractive to the glory of God. (PF, p. 181; italics in the original, verse in brackets added for clarity.

You can read the paragraph again, but one concept has been changed:

Damnation is only possible because of the divine purpose. The divine purpose flows from the Sovereign, who "works all matters after the counsels of His will." This confession is Christian: God is sovereign over all. There is no exclusion, and it is clear that human damnation falls within the realm God's "all things" will. God does all things according to His will, even His predestination of men and women for damnation. (Ephesians 1:22) repeats a fundamental truth: the glory of God is all that is in damnation. A biblical teaching does not include any teaching that is in any way detractive to the glory of God. (PF, p.181 - the underlined words are mine).

(Calvin) "And Augustine, tracing or tracing the origin or beginning of

Election to the free and unrestricted will of God places reprobation in His simple will as well. (EPG, p. 23)

God created angels and men for His glory. It is His glory that He saves some through grace. And it is for His glory, that He eternally condemns some to display His justice and glory. Calvin will discuss the ways God holds man responsible, so that God can condemn him to hell.

Calvin: "I get thereby the following conclusion, that God's mercy is offered equally to believers and those who don't believe, so those who do not believe are only made inexcusable and not saved." (EPG, p. 79)

(Calvin) "But how is it (saith Augustine), that God bestows grace, making some vessels of wrath according to their just desert and making others vessels of grace according to His grace; if we want to ask how this works, the only answer is this: "Who hath known God's mind?"

Lord?"' (EPG, p. 115 - 116)

This is grace! R.C. R.C. "Effective grace" is grace that affects what God wants. (CBG, p. 123)

Calvinistic grace is not best described as irresistible grace. When Calvin says that Georgius is an opponent to Calvin, he means:

Calvin: "The monk must then be forced to believe that faith should be common to all people by this argument. This, as we have previously abundantly demonstrated, is directly against the mind of the apostle Paul. The monk will continue his argument by stating that the elect have, according to our doctrine, "come short the glory of God." How does he arrive at his conclusion? He says that the grace of Christ is pouring out on all sinners. However, I believe the grace of God is universal and that the great difference lies in the fact that not all are called "according to God's purpose." (EPG, p. 150, underline mine).

(R.C. (R.C. Calvinists believe that man can and does resist God's grace. God's grace can be resisted in the sense that it is possible to resist it. It's irresistible when it accomplishes its purpose. It achieves God's desired result. I prefer the term "effectual grace." (CBG, page 120 - 121. - Abridged. Original italics - mine.

Grace from God is universal and accomplishes its purpose. Grace has always the effect God wants it to have on the recipient of this "unmerited favour". Grace has the effect of salvation on the elect: Only by God's grace can any man go to heaven. The result of grace on the reprobates is damnation. It is only through the grace of God that anyone can go to hell. God created man for His glory. Some men are saved for the glory of God, while some are condemned to hell for God's glory.

This "effectual grace" can't be resisted and is given to men according to God's will. Some are irresistible given saving effectual grace, while others are irresistibly granted damning effectual grace. Christ died for those whom God chooses to save. Grace gives the gift of faith to those who are unconditionally chosen. Man cannot choose God without the gift of faith because he is completely depraved. Grace is universal but the gift of faith and trust is not. All who are saved by grace and given faith are eligible to vote:

"His eternal selection of sinners was not determined by any pre-determined act or response from those chosen, but was solely based on His good pleasure and sovereign will." This election was not determined or conditioned on anything men might do. It was entirely God's purpose. (Five Points, p.

30)

White asserts that predetermination can be done "independently of knowing future events or, better yet, independent of any other than His sovereign and perfect will and purposes." (PF, p.67 - underlined by me - italics original) Grace is not required to save anyone. (CBG, 37) Man must be completely depraved. God must have created man in order to bring glory to Himself. Totalement inability means that man cannot choose God, and must have faith and regeneration before believing.

It is crucial to comprehend the chronology of Calvinistic events

Soteriology and the three meanings of faith:

Reformed theology teaches that:
1. (Sproul) "We don't believe to be born again, we are born again so that we can believe." (CBG, p. 73) 2. Faith is not universal:

Calvin: "This argument must drive the monk to the necessity to make faith common to all men." This, as we have seen, is in direct contradiction to the mind and intent of Paul. (EPG, p. 150; my underlined is mine).

3.   Faith is the gift from God:(Calvin:). "Augustine adds that faith, therefore, from its origin to its perfection, is the gift God. This gift is not given to all, but only those who are willing to fight the strongest testimony of Scripture will be able to deny that it is. The believer should not be concerned about why faith isn't given to everyone. He knows that all men were condemned by the sins of one. Calvin, EPG 21 - my underlined text

4. Regeneration precedes faith:
                    (Calvin:) "Hence it follows that first, faith does not
        proceed

"From within ourselves, but it is the fruit and result of spiritual regeneration." (Calvin's Commentary John 1:13)

5. Faith causes regeneration:
Calvin: "When the Lord breathes faith in us, He regenerates

We are adopted by a method that is secret and unknown to us. But after receiving faith, we feel a vibrant feeling of conscience and we see not only the grace of adopting, but also the newness of life, and other gifts of God.

Spirit." (Calvin's Commentary to John 1:13)

Faith is the catalyst for regeneration. But regeneration precedes faith. To avoid confusion, it is important to use the exact meaning of the word "faith". Faith is the ability to believe. Total Depravity, also known as Total Inability, is a state of total inability. Man must be given faith -- the gift of believing. Calvin: "I also affirm the gift of God's ability to believe in Christ." (EPG, p.149 - my underlined) Calvinism's second meaning of faith is "the act or believing".

(Sproul) "A fundamental point of Reformed Theology is the maxim "Regeneration precedes belief." Our nature is so corrupt and the power of sin too great that we won't choose Christ if God doesn't do a supernatural work in us. We don't believe to be born over again. We believe so that we believe. (CBG, pp. 72 - 73)

Faith is the gift of faith > Regeneration > Faith

"believing"

All men are completely depraved. They lack faith, the ability to believe. Man is regenerated when he is given faith, the ability to believe. Faith precedes regeneration. However, regeneration precedes faith. Believers are able to regenerate themselves, which in turn leads to believing. These are the three sections from Calvin's commentary John 1:13 with the explanation in parentheses:

(Calvin) "Hence it follows that first, faith (believing), does not

Proceed from within, but it is the fruit and result of spiritual regeneration. The Evangelist asserts that faith is a heavenly gift. Faith (the ability to believe in God) is a gift from God. Second, faith is not a bare or unrefined knowledge. Only those who have been renewed by God's Spirit can believe.

(Calvin) "It is possible to think that the Evangelist reverses nature by making regeneration precede faith (believing), but it is actually an effect of (the gift) faith (the ability) and should therefore be placed later. Both statements are perfectly compatible, because we receive the incorruptible seeds (1 Peter 1:23) through which we are born to a new, divine life.

 Yet, faith (believing), is an act of the Holy Spirit who dwells only in the children of God. In many ways, faith (the ability to believe) is part of our regeneration. It also allows us to enter the kingdom of God so that we may be counted among His children. Our renewal is the illumination of our minds by God's Holy Spirit. Faith (believing), therefore, flows from regeneration as its source. But since Christ sanctifies us through His Spirit by the same (gift) faith, it is also said that it is the beginning of our adoption. (My Note: Please see #1 below.

Calvin: "Another, simpler solution may be offered. For when the Lord breathes faith (the ability) into us, He regenerates by some method that is unknown and hidden to us. But after receiving faith (the ability), we feel a vibrant feeling of conscience not only the grace to adopt, but also the newness of life, and other gifts from the Holy Spirit. Since (the gift) faith (the ability believe) is received by Christ, it makes us a part of His blessings. In so far as our sense is concerned, we become the sons and daughters of God only when we have believed. (My Note: Please see # 2) If the inheritance of eternal live is the result of adoption, then we can see that the Evangelist attributes the entire of our salvation to Christ alone. And, indeed, no matter how carefully men examine themselves, there will be nothing that is worthy for the children of God except the gift Christ has bestowed upon them. (Commentary on John 1:3 - the words in parentheses were my addition, and underlined is mine.

1.   Faith is the foundation of our adoption, and adoption precedes regeneration:Calvin: "And from wherece is this gift to regeneration, but from God's free adoption?" (EPG, p. 100)

2.   Calvin: "God considers worthy of adoption those who believe in His Son but have been conceived by His Spirit. That is, those whom He has made for Himself to be His sons. If (the gift) of faith (the ability believe) makes us sons of God then the next question is: Where did faith (the ability believe) come? Who is the one who gives it? It is the fruit from the seed of God, which God gives again to new life. (EPG, pp. 44 45 - my addition is in parenthesesWhen the gift of faith and adoption is granted, man can be made a son by God.

Given that belief causes regeneration, we can only "sense" we are now the sons and daughters of God when we use that faith to believe. Before we believed, God made us sons. We only realize this when we believe. Then, we begin to behave like a child of God and become a son.

Luther and Calvin don't mean that man can be saved by believing in Christ without works when they say "sola fide", which is faith alone. This would make believing pre-regeneration and justification. These people believe that man is saved through the gift of faith, the ability to believe -- when God gives it. The gift of faith alone is sufficient to justify man. This justification occurs when faith is granted, not when faith is used. Because faith is the act of believing and being justified, salvation can only be based on works. Faith alone is sufficient to save man. Man is made alive, saved, justified and adopted by God. He is also made willing to believe. All this takes place before "faith," which refers to any believing done by elect.

(White:) "The gift (is) of repentance (is given) to the elect in

regeneration." (PF, p.149 - my addition is in parentheses)

Look back at the definition of Total Decreasingy:

Five Points: "Because the fall, man cannot save himself by believing the gospel. The sinner is dead, blind and deaf to God's truths; his heart is corrupt and deceitful. His will is not in freedom, it is bound to his evil nature. Therefore, he cannot -- and will not -choose the good over evil in this spiritual realm. It takes more than the Spirit's help to bring sinners to Christ. It takes regeneration, where the Spirit gives the sinner a new nature and makes him alive. Faith is not something that man can contribute to salvation, but it is a part God's gift for the sinner and not the sinner's gift. (The Five

Points of Calvinism, page 16 (underline mine).

Faith (believing in God) is not something man can contribute to salvation. Man is already saved through the gift of faith (the ability and willingness to believe). Faith (the ability or willingness to believe) is the first step in salvation.

"By grace, you have been saved by faith. This is not

It is your own work.

"May boast." Ephesians 2:8 - 9 (ESV)

Calvin: "And here we have to point out a very common error when it comes to the interpretation of this passage. Many people limit the meaning of gift to faith. Paul is merely repeating the former sentiment. He is not implying that faith is a gift from God but that salvation is given by God to us. (Commentary on Ephesians 2:18)

White: "There is no reason to accept that two of three substantival elements, grace and salvation, are a "gift," and faith is strictly a human contribution. Paul's whole theology, which includes the specific reference to faith being something that is "granted to us" (Philippians 1:29) would suggest that all three elements constitute a single gift of God. Surely grace is His to freely offer; salvation is His freely give; and likewise, saving faith is the gift God gives to His elect. (PF, p.296 - quotes and parentheses in original, mine).

White is the best person to explain what Calvin was saying. God's gift of grace is when God grants man the gift to salvation. He also gives him the gift of faith, which is the ability to believe. God does not give man the right to choose whether he gives grace, faith, or salvation. Man cannot deny the gift of faith, and the gift that God has given him of salvation. Grace, faith and salvation are the foundation of any belief made by man.

Calvin: "The next question is how do men receive the salvation offered by God to them? He concludes that faith is the only way to receive salvation. If salvation is not given to us by God's grace alone, or if we bring only faith, which takes us away from all praise, then it is grace alone. (Commentary on Ephesians 2:18 - italics in the original)

Men receive salvation only through faith. Therefore, salvation is not ours. God grants man faith only by grace. Man can bring nothing other than the gift God has given to him. God only gives the one type of faith: "Saving faith." To be saved you don't need to believe. God must give you the gift and grace of faith. You will then see that you are saved and will believe. Calvin: "The Evangelist states that all who believe in God are already born of God." (Commentary on John 1:12) Calvin again insists that to be made a son by God, one must have the gift of faith. This is the ability to believe. It precedes faith.

The forgiveness of sins (justification), is what brings about new life.

(regeneration). Man is not born to believe in order for him to believe. Is it possible to believe that we are born in sin again when we are reborn from the above? Is it possible to believe that our sins are not forgiven after we are adopted by God and made a son? We have to wait until we are made a son to be forgiven for our sins?

Calvin taught me that the answer to all these questions is

"no". This means that justification occurs in regeneration and precedes any believing done by man. If man believed before justification, it would mean that his salvation is dependent on his will. Or justification must precede faith (believing), or the will of the man, even if it agrees with God, has something to do the salvation of the man. This is contrary to what Calvin taught:

Calvin: "For if salvation of men is dependent on the mercy only of God, and if God saves no one but those He chooses by His secret good pleasure, then there can be absolutely nothing for men to do.

Will, or determine, salvation. Calvin agrees with this

conclusion (EPG, 48):

Calvin: "A little later, the same Augustine said, "Those who are predestined, called, justified and glorified by God are children of God; not just before they are regenerated but also before they are born from women; and such cannot perish." (EPG, p. 24, underlined mine).

This illustrates how the four main points of Calvinism are interconnected: Total Depravity (Unconditional Election), Limited Atonement (Limited Atonement), and Irresistible grace (Irresistible Grace). All four must be correct if any of these are true. All four of these must be incorrect if any one of them is wrong.

=

CHAPTER SEVEN

~

Reformed Theology Foundation / Calvinism:
1.   God can overrule the decisions of any of His creatures.
   2.   A. God is OmniscientB. God is OmnipotentC.

3.   A. God knew that the fall would occur.

4.   God could have stopped the fall from happening.God didn't have to create anything.The fall was willed, preordained and decreed by God.

5.   There is no free will in angels or men.

6.   It is God's will that it be done. > Created for God's Glory.

7.   Man doesn't know what good looks like.

8.   Total Depravity, Total Inability. > Three definitions of faith.

9.   Unconditional election. > Predetermination independent ofForeknowledge.

10.   Limited Atonement. > God is able to save all. He will save everything Jesus died for.

11.   Irresistible Effectual Grace > Grace universal

12.   The perseverance of the Saints. > Those who "fall from faith" are never saved.---------------------

The last chapter described the sequence of events that Calvin believed led to salvation. Faith is the cause of regeneration, which leads to faith. Augustine, Luther and Calvin refer to it as the first "faith", when they state that justification can be achieved only through faith:

A. The gift of faith is:Adoption

B. Make him a son of God

C. Given a new heart

D. Made alive

E. Recognize the gift of repentance

F. Born Again

G. Salvation

H. Justification

I. Redemption

J. Regeneration

1. To sense that he is saved, man uses the faith he just received. And, of course, man "believes".Calvinists can be trusted to say that the reformed view on salvation is "monergistic".

R. C. Sproul explains:

(Sproul) "When we claim that regeneration is monergistic we mean we

This means that only one party does the work. This party is God, the Holy Spirit. He regenerates us. We cannot do it by ourselves, or even assist Him in the task. (CBG, pp. 117 - 118)

It is important to determine whether the reformed monergism view is "coercive" and "persuasive". Calvinists argue first that man cannot come to Christ and must be "compelled" to do so. They then argue that no one is being dragged into heaven. Because coercion is external, and God's work on man is internal, regeneration is "persuasive".

R. C. Sproul explains how God can save everyone:

(Sproul) "Certainly God has the power to change your heart."

He will take every impenitent sinner into His arms and make them His. He cannot be sovereign if He does not have such power. Why doesn't He use that power for all? (CBG, p. 35)

Sproul continues to describe God as violating man's will:

(Sproul:) "The question still remains. Why is God able to save only some people? If God can save men through their wills, then why doesn't He violate everyone's will to bring salvation? (CBG, p. 36 emphasis mine).

(Sproul:) "The only thing I can answer to this question is that it's not clear to me. I don't know why God saves certain people but not others. While I do not doubt that God can save all, I also know that He doesn't choose to save everyone. I don't understand why.

One thing I know. If God pleases, He will save some but not all.

There is nothing wrong in that. God does not have to save anyone. God can save some people, but not all. The Bible reiterates that God has the divine right to show mercy on those whom He will. (CBG, p. 37; underlined mine).

This is the "mystery" of the Reformed faith. Why does a God who can force everyone into salvation choose not to? This mystery goes beyond why God chose Jacob to hate Esau. It also explains why God chose Pat to hate Jamie. You can substitute any name you wish.

R. C. Sproul persists in his belief that regeneration is more important than believing:

(Sproul) "The Reformed view on predestination teaches that

Before a person can choose Christ, his heart must change. He must be born again. (CBG, p. 72)

(Sproul). "One doesn't first believe, then become born again."

Then, be led into the kingdom. (CBG, p. 72)

(Sproul) "A key point in Reformed Theology is the maxim

"Regeneration precedes belief" (CBG, p. 72)

(Sproul) "We don't believe in order not to be born again. We are."

"Born again for the purpose of believing." (CBG, p. 73)

"And you were dead in your trespasses, sins in which once you

walked." Ephesians 2:1 - 2a (ESV)

"No one can get to me except the Father who sent him draws."

him. "And I will raise him up the last day." John 6:44 (ESV).

R. C.Sproul on John 6:44:

(Sproul) "The Greek term used here is Elko. Kittel's Theological Dictionary of the New Testament defines it as "to compel by irresistible superiority." The word "to compel" is a linguistic and lexicographic term. (CBG, p. 69 – underlined is mine - original italics) R. C. Sproul discusses either total depravity/total inability:

(Sproul) "Paul claims the man is dead. He is not drowning.

He has already fallen to the bottom of sea. It is futile for a man to give a life saver to someone who has already drowned. Paul says that God plunges into the sea to pull a drowning man out of the water. Then, he performs a miraculous act of mouth-to–mouth resuscitation. He breathes new life into the dead man. (CBG, p. 116)

Calvin agrees to Augustine and Sproul's view that drawing is compelling:

     (Calvin) "Christ also here proclaims, through this His
  doctrine that

 The ones who are "compelled" by God's will to draw others to Him will be
the most effective. (EPG, 34 - in quotation marks

 Calvin describes monergistic conversion and also describes repentance as
God's work in regeneration:

Calvin: "Whether repentance is His work or not, should not be in dispute.
Augustine's statement is so evidently correct: "Those whom God wills to
convert, He converts Himself." This includes making willing ones out of
those who were unwilling and also making sheep out of wolves and martyrs
from persecutors, thus transforming them.

 His all-powerful grace." (EPG, p.63 - italics original)

 Calvin describes the sequence of events in faith and describes man being
made to believe it:

Calvin: "Therefore, if faith is the fruit of Divine election it is immediately
evident that not all are enlightened or regenerated unto faith. It is therefore a
fact that God chose to bestow faith (the ability to believe) on those He
determined to do so. Augustine's sentiments are therefore truthful. He writes
that the elect of God were chosen by Him to be His Children, so that they
could be made believe, not because He knew they would believe. " (EPG,
page 145 italics and original - words are mine - underline mine).

 Monergism begins with God allowing you to believe against your will.
The elect are given the gift of faith against their will and they are compelled
by God to be saved. White and Calvin explained the reform interpretation of
Ephesians 2:18-9: Man is granted the gift, Grace, of Salvation. When man is
given Faith, the gift is Grace. These gifts are the source of regeneration. They
are given to man before he can receive the gift of faith. This regeneration

allows man to see that he is saved and to use the faith he was given to believe. The gift of faith is only available to those who believe.

R. C. Sproul: "If God does not have the right to coercion, then He doesn't have any."

He has the right to govern His creation." (CBG, p. 42)

R. C. Sproul: "Is it possible to receive grace of

Regeneration and faith still not found.
Calvinists respond emphatically with "No!"

It is misleading to use the term irresistible grace. Calvinists believe that man can and does resist God's grace. The question is "Can the grace that regenerates fail to fulfill its purpose?" Keep in mind that even though they are spiritually dead, they are biologically still alive. They have a disinclination to God. They will resist grace and do everything they can to stop it. Israel's history is one of a stubborn and hard-nosed people who repeatedly rejected God's grace.

God's grace can be resisted in the sense that it is possible to and does resist us. It's irresistible when it accomplishes its purpose. It achieves God's desired result. I prefer the expression effectual grace.

This is the grace of regeneration. That is what we remember.

God instills in us the desire to be like Him in regeneration. We will function the same way we have always functioned until we have this desire in us. Then we can make our decisions according to the strongest motivation. We will follow the example of Christ if God gives us that desire. We will almost certainly choose Christ as the object of our desire. We become spiritually awake when God makes us spiritually active. God does not create the possibility of spiritually living. God creates spiritual life in us. When He calls it into existence, it becomes real."

(Sproul:) "We refer to the inward calling of God. The inward calling of God is just as powerful and effective than His call to create the universe. God didn't invite the creation of the world. God gave the command to call out "Let there is light!" It was indeed light. It couldn't have been any other. It was time for the light to shine.

Could Lazarus have stayed at the tomb with Jesus calling him?

out? Jesus cried, "Lazarus, come forth!" The man escaped from his grave and emerged from the tomb. God can create, but only God can. Only He can bring life and create something from nothing. (CBG, pp. 120 -121 - italics, quotes in original, Abridged

Calvin explained that grace from God is universal:
Calvin: "I believe the grace of God is universal. The great difference lies in the fact that not all are called 'according God's purpose. " (EPG. p. 150 - quotes and italics in original).

Man is free to choose Christ if he is saved against his will. The grace of God and His gift are incomparable. The elect are "made to believe". This is similar to a man being forced to jump out of a plane five hundred feet above the ground without a parachute. The man is free to choose to fall to his death. This analogy shows that the man is already saved even before he is thrown off the plane.

R. C.Sproul agrees that man must believe. He then begins to argue for the persuasiveness of this compulsion. Recall that any belief made by man precedes redemption:
(Sproul) "The graces of God operate on the heart in such an way

so that the once unwilling sinner becomes willing. Because he is willing to choose Christ, the redeemed person chooses Christ. Because God created a new spirit in the person, the person will now choose Christ. God transforms an opposing will and removes the heart's hardness. (WTB, pp. 65 - 66)

R. C. Spull: "Calvinism doesn't teach, and has never taught, that God brings people running into the kingdom. Or has ever excluded anyone who wants to be there. The biblical teaching about man's spiritual death is the central point of the Reformed doctrine on predestination. Natural man doesn't want Christ. If God places a desire in his heart for Christ, he will want Him. Christ-followers don't come screaming and kicking against their wills once they have that desire. They want to be there. They want Jesus. They run to the Savior. Rebirth is the key to irresistible grace. It makes it possible for someone to be brought back into spiritual life, and Jesus can now be seen in all His irresistible sweetness. Jesus is irresistible for those who have been made alive by the things of God. Every soul that longs to be redeemed by the living Christ, is one whose heart beats with God's life. All who the Father gives Christ to come to Christ (John 6;37). (CBG, pp. (CBG, pp.122-123 - my underline is mine). I agree with Sproul about the fact that Calvinists don't believe God takes people kicking-and- screaming to heaven. This is the correct answer to a different question. Is Calvinism teaching that God forces man to accept salvation and faith, or is this a contradiction to his will? Calvinism teaches that God can do anything to violate man's will? Calvinism teaches that God compel man to be regenerated. Is God able to force man into making his own choice? Calvin and Sproul both teach that the answer is "yes" to all of these questions.

R. C. Sproul: "We have already demonstrated that Jesus explicitly and

It is clear that God has drawn man to enable him to reach Him. (CBG, p.74 - keep in mind that draw is "to compel with irresistible superiority"

Calvin: "For if salvation depends only on God's mercy, and if God saves only those He chooses by His secret good pleasure, then there is nothing men can do, will or decide in the matter salvation." (EPG, p. 48)

If belief precedes justification, then salvation is dependent on the will of the individual. Teaching that man can be "made to believe" means that belief precedes justification. This contradicts the notion that man has nothing "to do,will, or determine in the matter salvation".

Calvinism says that the elect are "forced", "forced", or "compelled" to regenerate. The elect believe that after regeneration they have been justified and adopted by God, made righteous, given the gift of salvation. The elect then chooses to believe in God. Calvinists don't believe that the elect can choose to believe in God. It's the exact opposite. God gives the gift of salvation and faith to the elect in order that they will believe in God. The elect are granted faith against their will, and then regenerated against them. The elect will then realize that they have been saved and will choose to believe God.

(R. C. Spull:) "We conclude the fallen man is still free to

He can choose what he wants, but his desires are only evil and he is unable to see the good news of Christ. He will not choose Christ if he is still in the flesh and unregenerate. Because he is unable to act against his will, he can't choose Christ. He does not desire Christ. He can't choose what he doesn't want. His fall is terrible. It is so severe that only God's effectual grace can bring him back to faith.

(CBG, p. 75)

Another Calvinist, B. B. Warfield, also addressed this issue. In this next quote, Warfield is agreeing with an article written by Miss Havergal, and arguing against an article written by Mr. Trumbull. Warfield agrees that everything that has to do with salvation is done by God, that the faith that

saves us is from Him. Warfield disagrees with any believing being done by
man at the initial point of salvation:

>   (Warfield) "Miss Havergal" refers to the wonderful
> passage

This allusion is made to inform her readers that God is wholly in control,
that He alone saves us, that salvation is our faith that binds us to our
Saviour, and that everything that enters into it comes from Him and Him
alone. Trumbull's teaching clearly states that believing in oneself is what we
do, and God and Christ are unable to help us unless we open the door. We
cannot trust Him with a trust we don't have to exercise in order for Him to
act upon us. (Perfectionism, pp. 366 - 367)

B. B. Man is forced to accept salvation/justification as his first point.

It is a gift you can't refuse:

(Warfield:) "Man does not have a part in salvation; and if he did, he would
not be able to do it. His very nature as a sinner, is that he feels helpless, that
is, "lost." This is why he is so active in the salvation process. God only
works in him the will and the doing according His good pleasure. "God does
not force salvation on any man," it is false. Although it would be more
accurate to state that salvation is not available to all men, the truth would
still be there. It is false that the "eternal Life in Christ Jesus our Savior" is a
"free gift from God". We have the option to accept or reject the offer.
Although our wills are completely free, they are extremely biased towards
its rejection. They will reject any offer that is not an "offer" as long as it's
not. It is false that God's gift of eternal life is an "offer". It is a "gift" and not
something He gives. We can accept or reject it as we wish, but God "gives"
it. Like He gave life to Lazarus, and wholeness for the man with the
withered arm. It was not within the power or Lazarus's power to reject -- or
accept -- the gift Christ gave to him. Nor is it in the power and ability of
dead souls rejecting life, or "accepting" it when God "gives it to them. God

is one we can trust. He gives life to the dead, and commands things that aren't as though they were. (Perfectionism, page 392 - mine underline)

- quotes in original)

After explaining how regeneration is against man's will and is done by compulsion Sproul will argue that this coercion does not work but is persuasive:

(Sproul) "To say we choose according to what is most appealing to us at the time is to say we choose what we want. We are always free to choose from any point we want. Self-determination is not the same as determinism. External forces can force us to do certain things. Determinism is a form of determinism. As we've seen, external forces can severely limit our choices, but they don't have to eliminate all options. They can't make us feel guilty about the things we don't like. If that happens, and hatred turns into delight, it's a matter for persuasion and not coercion. I can't be forced to do the things I enjoy doing. (CBG, p.59 - italics original)

The Law of the excluded middle is the third rule of logic: it can be either A or Non-A. It is God or not God that we are referring to. A person can choose to be forced or free. It can't be both free and forced at the same moment and in the same way.

Sproul claims that there are two actions within this description and not one act. This is to circumvent the law of the excluded middle. God coerces the elect to be restored. The elect choose God. Calvinists disagree with the idea that God makes anyone choose Him. The elect "willingly believe" God once God has made them willing.

Arguments are made that grace is an inner force and not an external force. However, the grace that makes man willful comes from God, not man. This means that this grace must have come from outside of man even though it doesn't begin to work until it's inside him. This reasoning would suggest that capital punishment by lethal injection is not coercive but persuasive since the chemicals affect the internal organs. Jack Kevorkian would be innocent if he said that the analogy is not true because the prisoner doesn't want to die.

Calvinists don't believe man is dragged kicking-and- screaming to heaven. Calvinists believe man is dragged kicking-and- screaming to salvation, justification and regeneration when the gift, faith, is given against his will. The cause (the gift and regeneration of faith) and the inevitable effect (belief), are coercive. This means that the effect is forced upon the victim. C. S. Lewis vehemently rejects Sproul's argument:

(Lewis) "Again, freedom must refer to freedom for a creature."

Choose: This implies that there are many things you can choose from.

(POP, p. 380)

The following lament from Jesus could have two meanings:

Matthew 23:37 How many times would I have brought your children together like a hen gathers her brood beneath her wings? (ESV – underlined is mine

Calvinism would have Jesus said, "How often would I have gathered you children together like a hen gathers her brood beneath her wings?".

I hope you will be able to understand why Calvinism believes that "coercive monergism", rather than "persuasive monoergism" is the best way for me to explain it. Modern Calvinists are unlikely to agree with Calvin regarding "justification by faith alone". During the Reformation, the view was that justification occurred in the first faith. Modern Calvinists believe that justification occurs after believing or the second faith. This is why Sproul explains that man chooses Jesus after regeneration, which makes salvation convincing. White supports both of these views:

White: "This is the soil that springs the Reformed emphasis on sola fide (faith alone), the truth that one's justification is not through any meritorious work or action but by faith alone in Jesus Christ. When the foundation of the

Reformation is broken, one cannot claim to be faithful. The message of the gospel is the truth that God saves Himself by His own power and His own will.

Reformers." (PF, p. 36. Italics and quotes in the original

White begins by describing justification through believing in Jesus, which is the second faith of the reformed formula. This would mean that justification doesn't happen in regeneration, since belief precedes justification. White then agrees with Calvin that God does all things. This indicates that justification is caused and occurs in regeneration. Coercive monergism is the first. It is against man's will and without his choice. Coercive monergism is the second, as there is no way to respond. It is unclear how clear Sproul could make it that regeneration does not allow man to respond in the right way. It is unclear how much more clear Sproul could be that man does not have the ability to react in a certain way after regeneration. Man must believe.

We are now left to wonder what man's salvation ability is. Are we completely depraved and unable to choose God or do we have an impaired capacity to choose God.

R. C. Sproul explains Calvinist views very succinctly in a chart found on p. 66, Chosen By God: Post-Fall Man: "able and unable to sin".

Calvin agreed with this quote: (Calvin) "Whereas they have heaped bad deeds upon bad deeds throughout the course of their lives, since, being essentially sinful by their sinful birth, they could not do anything else than sin. They sinned not outwardly or from any constraint but knowingly and willingly. No one would deny that nature's corruption and depravity are the sources and fountains of all sins. If you ask me why God forgives sin in his elect and doesn't consider the reprobate deserving of the same remedy, I will tell you that the answer lies in Him. (EPG, p. 101. Underlined by me - original in italics)

Calvin: "There is no desire to do good in men."

they are not a result of God's selection." (EPG, p. 127)

"All have turned aside; together they have become worthless; no one is righteous; no one understands; and no one seeks God. They have all turned their backs; they are now worthless together; no one does good, even one." Romans 3:10 - 12

(ESV – underlined is mine

Calvinists define "nobody does good" as "nobody does any vertical or personal good." Norman Geisler agrees with James White that this is a good description of what Calvinists read in Romans 3:10-12:

(White:)

They are good, but, according to extreme Calvinism they are completely incapable of initiating, achieving, or ever receiving salvation without God's grace. (CBF, p. 57 – Quoted in PF. p. 100).

Romans addresses the ability of man vertically or spiritually to do good:
"For the wrath is revealed from Heaven against all ungodliness of men, and unrighteousness. They know what they can learn about God because God has revealed it to them. Since the creation of the universe, God's invisible attributes, His eternal power, and His divine nature, are clearly visible in all things. They have no excuse. They knew God but did not give Him thanks or honor Him as God. Their foolishness was a result of their inept thinking. Romans 1:18-21 (ESV – underline mine) Calvin offers a reformed interpretation of this passage:
Calvin: "It thus clearly appears what the consequences are of having this evidence -- men cannot allege any thing before God's tribunal in order to show that they are not wrongfully condemned. This is a crucial distinction. The manifestation of God in His creation is clear enough with respect to the

light; however, because of our blindness it is not sufficient. However, we are not so blind that our ignorance can be used as an excuse for our perverseness. We believe there is a God, and then we conclude that He should be worshipped. But our reasoning fails here because it can't determine who or what kind of God He is. The Apostle, Hebrews 11:3, says that faith is the only way man can attain real knowledge from the creation work. But our blindness prevents us from seeing the end. We still see enough that we don't have any excuse. (Commentary on Romans 1:10 - my underline)

Calvin says that although we may not see, we are still blind. Scripture says that they are blind but can see. Calvin states that the God they have seen plainly is not sufficient:
(Calvin:) "I, in turn, ask him why. If such be the case. God did."

Not command that the Gospel be preached to all people, indiscriminately from the beginning of the universe? (EPG, p. 151)

Paul, however, tells us that the opposite is true in Romans. "For His invisible attributes namely His eternal power, and divine nature have been clearly perceivable, ever since creation of the universe, in all things that have been made." Paul is stating that man can reason his way to God by what he has seen in God's creation and handiwork. This is why man is not excused. Man would be excused if the revelation of God through creation is not sufficient.

In Colossians, Paul tells us that the gospel was preached to everyone.

men:
"If you continue in the faith grounded, settled, and not move away from the hopeof the gospel, which you have heard, which was preached under heaven to every creature which is below it; whereof I Paul Am Made a Minister;" Col 1:23 (KJV).

(Calvin:) "He also adds, besides and a confirmation thereof, that it is exactly the same as was preached throughout the entire world." (Calvin's comment on Colossians 1:23)

Calvin on the complete inability of reprobates to understand the gospel:

Calvin: "What is free will?" The Scriptures all declare that man is the captive, servant, or slave of devil and is taken away into wickedness with all his mind and inclination, making him utterly incapable of understanding and even doing the things of God. (EPG, p.192 - italics are in the original - my underline is mine).

Calvin's clearest definition is Total Depravity: Man is completely incapable of understanding God's things. The reprobate cannot see God in His creation, so God showing it to them is equally evil. Calvin said that man can "see" or "clearly see" God. This shows that belief in total inability to perceive and understand God is against scripture.

James White disagrees with Calvin and says that the reprobate can clearly see God in His creation, and even understand the Gospel. It is not clear how the reprobate who are unable to sin and cannot do any good, can be able to do this good and do it well:

White: "Calvinists certainly believe that unsaved persons can and do comprehend the truth of Gospel. However, they universally reject it beyond the divine act. (PF, p.118 - italics original)

This view of total depravity leads people to believe in exclusivism or restrictivism (See PF at p. 229). Calvin taught that the gospel is not preached for all people, Jesus died only for the elect and the gift of faith can only be given to them. Those who don't have the gospel preached cannot be saved. Salvation is limited to those God chooses for the gospel to be preached to and salvation is restricted only to those He graciously gives the gift of faith.

(Calvin) "Every sinner, either because of his faults, is inexcusable"

Original sin and sinful nature, or from an additional act of his will. It doesn't matter if he knew he was sinful, or not. It does not matter if he has a judgment of right or wrong. Inadvertence is sin in and of itself in those who don't understand; ignorance, on the other hand, is sin in those who do not understand. (EPG, p. 54)

This interesting Calvin statement on eternal destiny of infants leads to exclusivism: Some infants will eternally live, while others will be condemned to eternal damnation:

(Calvin) "But, original sin and guilt aren't, in the estimation

Pighius is sufficient to make men forever condemned. And if God cannot have a secret judgement of him, what will he do about infant children who are removed from this life before they can possibly perform any of the works mentioned above? There was the exact same natural condition of birth as death in both the infants who died at Sodom and those who died at Jerusalem. Their works, or lack thereof, were exactly the same. It is possible that Christ will in the final day separate the two, placing one on His right and the other on His Left. Who doesn't love the glorious judgment of

God, who ordered that one of these children should live at Jerusalem. From there, they could be taught the truth and be able to lead a better life. The other should be born in Sodom, the wide entrance into hell. (EPG, p. 99 - 100)

=

CHAPTER EIGHT

~

Foundation of Classical Theism:

1. God can give His creatures freedom at will.

2. A. A.

     B.   God is Omnipotent

     C.   God is Perfect

8.   A. God knew that the fall would occur.The fall could not be stopped by God.God didn't have to create anything.The fall wasn't ordained by God. God gave man the power to choose.Angels and man are "Free Moral Agents".It is true. Therefore, God wills it. (Man was created to love God.) 7. Man's ability to discern good from evil is limited.Unrighteous with impaired abilities > Faith - ability believe - common for all.

9.   According to Foreknowledge, Election is Predetermined

10.   All Atonement: Universal, Voluntary and Special, Penal, Substitutionary.

11.   Universal Resistible Grace > Every person is responsible for the amount of revelation received.

12.   The perseverance of the Saints. > Only the elect believe.-------------------

C. S. Lewis explains how God cannot do anything that is logically inconsistent, and that it is logically contradiction to claim that God can give man freedom while withholding freedom from him. C. S. Lewis explains how the doctrine of fall teaches that man is now a horror to God as well as to himself, and a creature ill adapted to the universe. This is not because God made him so, but because he made himself that way by the misuse of his free will. (POP, p. 397)

This means that God did not cause the fall, but instead angels and men have free will. The definition of free will is: It is free from external and internal coercion but not without persuasion and influences.

God's will flows from His Nature. There is an intrinsic right and wrong. God commands certain things because He knows they are right. God's will is determined primarily by His wisdom, which sees and His goodness, which embraces the intrinsically good. (POP, p. 409)

C. S. Lewis's Perelandra describes a new world that includes an Adam, Eve, a tempter and a Christ figure. Instead of living in a garden with forbidden fruits, the first couple live in floating mats of vegetation and cannot spend the night on any soil-covered island. Weston plays the role of the tempter. He was possessed by a demonic and supports the Calvinistic view that God willed that man sin in order to bring about the redemption of the fallen. This view is opposed by Ransom, Christ's figure.

Ransom addresses "the green woman", who represents "Eve". Ransom says:

(Lewis): "This man (Weston), has stated that the law against living is against the law

The Fixed Island Law is different than the other Laws because it isn't the same for all universes and because it doesn't have the same goodness. He says so far that it is all well. He then says it is so different that you might not obey it. There might be another reason.

(Lewis): "I believe He (God), made one law like that in order to have obedience. What you call obedience to Him in all of these other matters is doing what feels good in your eyes. Is that love? They are His will. But you don't have to do them because He commands. If He asks you to do something that is His will, where can you feel the joy of obeying? Perelandra, p. 101. The parenthetical words were my additions - the underline is mine.

The Green Lady responds:

(Lewis) "Oh, it's so clear to me!" Maleldil's can't be left!

God's will, but He has given us the ability to walk outside of His will. Without a command such as this, there would be no way to do so. We can do it by our own will. It's like stepping out from the earth's roof and into Deep Heaven. Love is all that exists beyond. "I knew that there was joy in seeing the Fixed Island, and I gave up all thoughts of ever living there. But I didn't understand it until now." (Perelandra, pp. 101 -102 - italics are in the original - my addition is in parenthetical words

This argument is quite simple. God makes a promise to man, like he will eat from any tree. God is bound by His nature. God gave Man free will. Who are you to question God? Calvinists believe that God ordered Joseph's brothers to sell him into slavery in Egypt for Him to bring good out of it. C. S. Lewis disagrees with the assertion that evil was God's will. However, he believes that God brought good out it:

        (Lewis) "Even God would tell him that goodness came of it."

Disobedience at the end. It was a good thing. Maleldil is a beast that can be stopped by His will, or a leaf we can bend His form? He will do what you ask. However, He will not bring you the good things He has planned for you if your obedience was perfect. This is gone forever. The forbidden thing was done by the first King and the first Mother of the world; He made it right in the end. We have yet to see what they lost. There were others to whom no good came or ever will come." Perelandra, page 104) The Abolition of Man provides an explanation for the Natural Law as well as intellectualism. This view holds that there is an intrinsic good or evil. This is the reason for creation:

        (Lewis) "We were not made to love God (though that is a part of our purpose), but so that God might love us and that we can be objects where the Divine love may be 'well-pleased'. (POP, p.

388 - Parentheses in original

James White quotes Charles Spurgeon's sermon, which is consistent in Calvinism's view that God created man to bring glory back to Himself:

(Spurgeon) "The doctrine of Divine Sovereignty is God's most comforting attribute. ... God will not be allowed to be anywhere except on His throne. When God ascends to His throne

His creatures then gnash and grumble; when we declare an enthroned God and His right, without consulting His creatures, to dispose His creatures as He pleases, it is that we are exacerbated and men listen to us. God on His throne, however, is not the God that they love. (PF, p. 36-37 - my underlined, Abridged).

C. S. Lewis might have thought of this sermon when he wrote The Magicians Nephew. He argued against Calvin's view that man was created to glorify God:

(Lewis) The Queen said that it was her fault. "She drove."

It is mine. Let the curse of all Powers be upon her forever! At any moment, I was ready for peace. She refused. Her pride has decimated the entire world. Even before the war began, there was a solemn agreement that neither side would use Magic. What could I do when she broke her promise? Fool! She didn't know I had more magic than her! She didn't know that I knew the secret to the Deplorable Wort. Did she believe she was weak? That I wouldn't use it? "What was it?" Digory said.

"That was the secret to secrets," declared Queen Jadis. It had

The great kings of our race knew for a long time that there was a word that, if used with proper ceremonies, would kill all living creatures except the person who said it. The ancient kings were weak and gentle-hearted, and they bound themselves and those who came after them with great oaths to never seek out the word's meaning. It was hard to find it and I paid a

horrible price for it. It was only when she forced it that I used it. I tried
every other way to defeat her. I poured out my army's blood like water --
"Beast!" Polly muttered.

"The last great war," the Queen said, "raged for three consecutive days here
in Charn." It was this exact spot that I watched for three days. I didn't use
my power until the last of my soldiers fell, and my sister, the accursed
woman at the head her rebels, was about halfway up the great stairs leading
up from the city up to the terrace. Then, I waited until we were close
enough to see each other's faces. I was stunned when she turned her evil,
wicked eyes on me, and said, "Victory." "Yes," I replied, "Victory, but it
was not yours." Then, I spoke the Deplorable Wort. "I was the only living
thing under the sun."

"But the people?" Digory gasped.

"What people, boy?" The Queen asked.

Polly said, "All the normal people" who had never done her any harm. The
women, the children, the animals.

"Don't you understand?" The Queen, still speaking to Digory, said: "I was
the queen." They were all my people. They were there to fulfill my will.

He said, "It was quite hard luck on them all the same.".
"I forgot that you were a common boy. How can you grasp the reasons for
State? It is important to understand, child, that the things that would be bad
for you or any other common person are not wrong for a great Queen like
me. Our shoulders carry the weight of the entire world. All rules must be
broken. We have a lonely and high destiny.

Digory suddenly remembered Uncle Andrew's use

They were exactly the same words. They sounded grander when Queen Jadis spoke them, perhaps because Uncle Andrew wasn't seven feet tall and dazzlingly gorgeous. (TMN, pp. (TMN, pp. 41-42 - my underline)

Calvin taught that God's glory is a mix of men who have been saved and sent to heaven and men who are condemned and sent to hell. Spurgeon preached this sovereign God. However, Irenaeus said that "The glory and power of God is man fully awake, and the life of God consists in seeing God" (Against The Heresy Of Gnosticism). It is difficult to see the contrast between man being created primarily to glorify God and man being created primarily so that God can love us. Opposite views on the Omni-benevolence and primary purpose of creation of man lead to opposing views. The belief that something is right, therefore God wills it leads to intellectualism. This opposes Calvinism's view on the man's ability.

Intellectualism is a belief that, even though man may not be righteous in God's sight, he still has the ability of knowing good from bad. The following passages are from Romans:

"As it is written: "None is righteous, no, not one; no one

All are understood; none seeks God. They have all turned their backs; they are worthless together; no one does good. Romans 3:10 - 12

(ESV)

"For what they can know about God is clear to them, because God

It has been shown to them. His invisible attributes, namely his eternal power, and his divine nature, are clearly visible in all things. They have no excuse. They knew God but did not give God thanks or honor him as God. Their thinking became futile and their foolish hearts darkened. Romans 1:19 - 20 (ESV)

Calvinists modify "nobody does good" to "nobody does spiritual good". Classical Theists modify "nobody does good" to "no-one always does good" or "no person is good enough," which is an extension of "None can be righteous". Classical Theists claim that this is in line with the context of the passage which is righteousness and harmonizes both passages. The natural law, which is the ability of man to distinguish right from wrong, does not allow him to see God in His creation. The ability to see God in His creation is a good thing. This means that anyone who sees God in His creation does spiritual good.

C. S. Lewis on Total Depravity:
(Lewis) "I disbelieve in that doctrine partly because it is logically wrong."

If our depravity was total, we shouldn't consider ourselves depraved. (POP, p. 395)

It is simple: Why do reprobates feel shame or guilt when they are completely depraved? Because they are aware of the law God has given them, they feel guilty when they disobey it. They can also reason their way to what is intrinsically good or evil. This argument is not easily dismissed by saying that "total depravity" means "utter depravity." Total depravity is a doctrine that says man cannot do anything good. The ability to recognize what is good means that man can do good.

In Out of the Silent Planet, C. S. Lewis describes the difference between a completely depraved and a fallen man. Weston is a fallen human capable of understanding good and bad. Devine, the "thin one", is completely depraved and unable to discern good from evil. Oyarsa, the good angel who rules the world where this conversation occurs, is Oyarsa. Earth is the Silent Planet:
(Lewis) "Oyarsa Weston: I see now how you have been bent by the lord in the silent world. All hnau (rational beings similar to man) are familiar with the laws of pity, straight dealing, shame, and the like. One of these laws is the love for one's fellow human. He taught you how to break every law except one. This one is not the greatest. He bent it until it became folly and

set it up in your brain, thus making it a little Oyarsa. You can only obey it now, even though you could give no other explanation for why it is a rule than the many other greater laws it forces you to ignore. Is this the reason he did it?

Weston to Oyarsa - "Me think not such person -- me smart, new

"Man, don't believe that old talk!"

Oyarsa Weston: "I'll tell you. Because a bent hnau is more evil than one that has been broken, he has left this one. He has only bent your hnau; but the Thin One, who sits on the ground that he has broken, because he has left nothing but greed. He is now a talking animal, and in my view he can do no more evil than any animal. If he was mine, I would make his body available to the hnau. If you were my Thick One, I would attempt to heal you. Tell me Thick One, how did you get here? (Silent, pp. 137-138 - Italics in Original, Words in Parentheses Added for Clarity

Geisler also opposes total inability, total depravity:
Geisler: "Sound Reason Demands That There Is No Responsibility

if they are unable to respond. It is absurd to hold someone accountable when they couldn't have responded. God is rational. (CBF, p. 29)

Reason is the basis of intellectualism. We have the ability to reason about what is intrinsically right or wrong. Fallen man would not feel guilt without this ability. The Divine attribute of justice would also prevent a completely depraved person from being held accountable by God. A completely depraved person cannot respond, and therefore is not responsible. Because he wouldn't know that he did anything wrong, a totally depraved person would not feel guilty about doing something wrong.

This view of man's depravity means that anyone can believe in God. All men have the ability to believe, which is called faith. Justification is preceded by faith, which can be defined as believing:

"For what is the Scripture saying? "Abraham believed God and

It was considered righteousness to him." Romans 4:3 (ESV)

"But what does it mean? "The word is close to you, in your lips and

"In your heart" refers to the word of faith we proclaim; because if you believe with your heart that Jesus is Lord, and confess that God raised him from death, you will be saved. One believes and is justified with the heart, while one confesses and gets saved with the mouth.

Romans 10:8 - 10 (ESV)

Luther, Calvin, and Augustine taught that faith (defined as the ability to believe) is the basis of justification. This was accomplished in regeneration. It preceded any belief being made by man. Their "justification through faith alone" was actually "justification through the gift of the ability (faith) alone". This justification occurs before any believing is done by man.

C. S. Lewis teaches that "justification through faith alone" is simply "justification through believing (faith). This view is compatible with the order described above in the verses.

Analyzing the different views on Alexander's salvation illustrates the implications for the belief that faith is common to all or that faith is only available to select people:

"This charge I entrust you, Timothy, as my child in accordance

With the prophecies that were made about you before, that you may wage good war, with faith and a good heart. Some have rejected this and have lost their faith. Hymenaeus, Alexander, and others have been handed to Satan so they can learn not to blaspheme. 1 Timothy 1:18 - 20 (ESV)

Calvinists believe faith is a gift from God, and only the elect are granted this gift. This gift also includes salvation. Therefore, Hymenaeus must have been saved. This conclusion is not compatible with Calvinism and requires a different meaning of faith.

Faith is the ability to believe.

The second definition is belief.

The third definition is sound doctrine.

Calvin explains 1 Timothy 1:18-20 in this way:

Calvin: "I understand faith to be a general expression, denoting sound doctrine. The treasure of sound doctrine is valuable, so we should not be surprised if it is taken away. Paul tells us that there is only one method to keep it safe. That is, by using the locks and bars that a good conscience can secure it. (Commentary on 1 Timothy 1:19, italics in the original).

Calvin continues to explain Alexander's fate and Hymenaeus' fate:

Calvin: "As I mentioned during the exposition of another passage (1 Cor. v. 5), there are those who believe that an extraordinary chastisement was given to these people. They view it as referring "to the powers" mentioned in Paul's Epistle. (1 Cor. 12:28). As the apostles were endowed the gift of healing, to prove the favor and kindness God has towards the godly, they were equipped with power against rebellious and wicked people, to either deliver them to the devil or inflict other chastisements. Peter and Sapphira were the first to witness this "power", while Paul was in the magician Barjesus. For my part, I prefer to explain it as relating the excommunication. The belief that the Corinthian incestuous received any other chastisement except excommunication isn't supported by any probable conjecture. If Paul excommunicated him and delivered him to Satan by doing so, then why shouldn't the same expression be used in this passage? It also explains the force of excommunication. For Christ is the head of the Church, and Satan rules the Church. Therefore, anyone who is excommunicated from the Church must be put for a while under the tyranny Satan until he returns to Christ. One exception is that he may have given them a sentence for perpetual excommunication because of the gravity of the offense. However, I wouldn't venture to assert that. (Commentary on 1 Timothy 1;20 - Parentheses original)

This passage is from Calvin's commentary and illustrates the difficulties Calvin encountered because he believed that faith was not common among all men. This means that only the elect receive faith, and "faith from its beginning until its perfection is the gift" of God.

God". This would indicate that God gave Hymenaeus an inferior gift because they "shipwrecked" their faith. It's no wonder Calvin struggled to understand the meaning of this scripture, and even pretended it was.

This scripture is explained by Classical Theists in a very simple way. Everyone has the ability to believe in something. In fact, everyone can put their faith in something. Everybody is worshipping something. This is how Hymenaeus, Alexander and others could lose their faith and be handed over to Satan by Paul. They did not lose the salvation they had because everyone has faith and not everyone is saved.

Believers that faith (the ability of believing) is shared by all men is contradictory to "total sin" and "total inability". It also seems to leave the ball in man's hands when it comes down to determining who is saved or condemned. Coercive Monergism was the Calvinist response to salvation being completely God's. Synergism is the Arminian answer. It states that God and man "work together" to save us. C. S. Lewis repeatedly advocates persuasive monergism.

C. S. Lewis teaches God is sovereign. Faith is a gift. Just as life, breathing and rain are gifts from God, so faith:

   (Lewis) "Our lives are, at all moments, supplied by Him.

The tiny, miraculous power that He gives us is only possible on bodies where His energy continues to exist. (POP, p. 386)

(Lewis) "All living things are created by God in the sense that

They were made by Him and are maintained in existence at all times. (Miracles, p. 303)

(Lewis) "But God's love is not caused by goodness in an object. He causes all the goodness that the object has, loving the object first into existence, and then into real, even if derivative, lovability. God is goodness.

He can give good but cannot get or need it. (POP, p. 389)

God made angels and man "free". God chose to make man responsible and to bind him by his salvation decision. This is Classical Theism's "mystery". Why Jamie believes and Sam doesn't believe. This view would lead one to believe that scriptures teach that God wants to save all people:

   "This is good and pleasing in the sight God our Savior.

Who desires for all people to be saved, and to know the truth. 1 Timothy 2:3 - 4 (ESV)

"Have you any pleasure in the death the wicked, declares God

GOD and not that he should live in obedience to his will? Ezekiel

18:23 (ESV)

"The Lord is not slow to fulfill his promises, as some men believe."

Do not count slaciness. But, it is longsuffering and willing to us-ward. C. S. Lewis summarizes it this way:

(Lewis) "If God speaks sometimes as though the Impassible might suffer passion and eternal fullness, and in need of those beings upon whom It bestows everything from their naked existence upwards, then this can only mean, if anything is intelligible to us, that God of mere miraculous has made Himself hungry and created in Himself that which can satisfy. The requirement He makes is His. If the immutable heart is able to be hurt by puppets of its own creation, it is Divine Omnipotence that has done so, free and with a humility that surpasses understanding. (POP, p. 389; my underlined text is mine). It is this freedom that allows you to give yourself back to him:

(Lewis) "The life of the good angels is also supernatural in another sense. This means that they have offered to God the 'natures He created'. There is an even higher type of 'life from God' that can only be granted to creatures who willingly surrender to it.

As with angels so with us. In the relative sense, every man's rational part is supernatural. This is the same way that both angels as devils are supernatural. If it is, according to theologians, "born again", if it gives itself over to God in Christ, then it will have an absolutely supernatural life, which is not created at any point but is begotten.

This is the only way to give an animal this Supernatural life. However, every creature that can think can receive it by voluntary surrendering to Christ's life.

Christian writers use the terms'spiritual and'spiritual,' to refer to the life that arises in rational beings who voluntarily give their will to Divine grace and become sons and daughters of the Heavenly Father in Christ. (Miracles, pp. (Miracles, pp.303-304 - italics original, Abridged).

Our response to Him is voluntary surrender. This "surrendering" is the precursor to regeneration or being "born again". It is coerced in that we are required to make a decision. It is free in that we can choose how our response or decision will affect us for better or worse:

(Lewis) "But to understand it as a love in the which we were primarily wooers and God was the wooed in, in that we sought and He found us, in the which His conformity and our needs came first, is to be ignorant of the true nature of things. We are creatures. Our role must be one of agent to patient, male to female, light to mirror, voice to voice. The highest activity we can do is respond, not invent. The only way to truly experience the love of God is to surrender to His call, to submit to His will. To experience it the other way is to be a solecism against His grammar. While I recognize that the soul may be searching for God on a certain level, and God may be perceived as being receptive to the souls' love, the soul's search can only be described as an appearance of God's search. All comes from Him. Our freedom is just a choice of better or worse responses. (POP, p. 389; my underlined is mine).

C. S. Lewis's teachings are, I believe, that God is sovereign. However, Divine Omnipotence can not do what is logically inconsistent: Force men to choose Him. God may desire that all be saved. However, not all will be saved. God cannot do what is logically contradictory by forcing men to choose Him and love him freely.

The law of noncontradiction: A cannot be non-A. Two contradictory statements cannot both be true in the same way and at the same moment. The law of the excluded middle is A or non-A. An act can be either free or forced.

"I tell you the truth, it is to my advantage that I go."

Don't leave, because if I don't go, the Helper won't come to you. If I go, he will come to you. He will bring the judgment on the whole world regarding sin, righteousness, and judgment. John 16:7-11 (ESV).

Persuasive monergism is the belief that every person has: Faith can be described as the ability to believe and a belief in someone or something. Every person is convinced or convict by the Holy Spirit. This conviction is against man's will. The Holy Spirit can convict man at his will. Man has no choice. The conviction "forces" man into making a decision. "Necessity might not be the contrary of freedom." (SBJ, p. 123)

The Holy Spirit convicts man of his sins by dragging him along. This is a matter of no choice. This conviction is binding on us. God freely chose to give each sinner the direction of their response to this conviction. C. S. Lewis called this "our freedom": "Our freedom is only a freedom to choose a better or worse response." (POP. p. 389) Man may continue to rebel by putting his faith in science, money, education, and himself. Man can either surrender, believe, or be justified and receive the gift that salvation is freely offered.

C. S. Lewis, in The Great Divorce describes what it would look like if people could travel to Hell from the edge of Heaven. He sees it from the perspective of a "ghost" who has traveled up to heaven on a bus:

(Lewis) "I saw a Ghost coming towards us who was carrying something on his shoulders. He was not substantial, like all Ghosts. But they were different from each other as smokes differ. One had been light and oily, while this one was darkened and oily. A little red lizard sat on his shoulders, twitching its tail as a whip, whispering in his ear. He turned his head towards the reptile as soon as he was visible, and he did so with an impatience-stricken grin. "Stop, I'm telling you!" He said. He continued to whisper to it as the tail wriggled. He stopped snoring and began to smile. He then turned around and began to walk westward away from the mountains.

"Off so soon?" A voice spoke.

Although the speaker was larger than average in size, he looked more human.

He was a man of such brightness that I couldn't look at him. His presence was a constant smack on my eyes, and my body (for heat came from him as well), like the dawn sun at the start of a hot summer day.

'Yes. The Ghost replied, "Yes. "Thanks for your hospitality. It's not worth it, you see. I said to this little chap (here he indicated that he was referring to the Lizard) that he would have to be quiet if they came, which he insistently did. His stuff won't work here, I know that. He won't quit. "I will just have to go home."

"Would it be okay for me to make him calm?" The flaming Spirit, an angel, replied.

Ghost replied, "Of course I would,".

The Angel took a step forward and said, "Then I will kill he.".

'Oh -- ah -- look out! You're burning my face. Keep away," said the Ghost, as he retreated.

"Don't want him to be killed?"

"You didn't mention anything about killing him at the beginning. I didn't mean to bother you with something so extreme as that.

"It's only way," said the Angel, whose burning fingers were now very close the Lizard. "Shall I kill it?"

"Well, that's another question. It's something I am open to considering, but it's still a new point. It's embarrassing.

'May I kill it?'
"Well, we'll have to talk about that later. There is not
enough time. Can I kill it? Please, it was not my
intention to be a nuisance. Don't bother! Look! It has
gone to sleep by itself. It'll be fine now, I'm certain.
Thanks ever so much.'

'May I kill it?'
"Honestly, I don't see the need for it. It's not something I can do right now. It would be better to continue the process than to kill it.

"The gradual process is useless."

"Don't you think so?" You're right. I will ponder what you have to say. I will. Actually, I would let you do it now. However, I am not feeling very well right now. It would be foolish to do it now. For the operation, I would need to be in good physical condition. Perhaps another day.

"There is no other day." All days are here now.

'Get back! You are burning me. You're burning me. You'd kill me if you did.' It isn't so.

"Why are you hurting me now?"

"I never said it wouldn't hurt you." It wouldn't kill me, I assured you.

"Oh, I know. You think I am a coward. It's not. It isn't. It's not, I swear! Let me get back on tonight's bus to get my opinion

doctor. I will be back the moment I can.

"This moment is the sum of all moments."

"Why are you torturing my? I am being mocked. You are tearing me apart. Why didn't I ask you to kill the damned thing before you could help me? If you hadn't, it would have been over by now.

"I cannot kill it against my will." It is impossible. It is impossible.

The Angel's hands were nearly closed on the Lizard but they weren't quite.

The Lizard started talking to the Ghost so loudly that I could not hear it.

It warned, "Be careful." He can do whatever he says. He can kill me. He will kill me with one fatal word. You'll then be without me for ever and ever. It is not natural. It's not natural. You would be a ghost and not as real as you are now. He doesn't understand. He is a cold, bloodless abstraction. While it may seem natural to him, it's not for us. Yes, yes. Yes, I do know that there are no real pleasures right now. Only dreams. Aren't they better that nothing? I promise to be even more good. Although I have admittedly been a bit too reckless in the past, I swear I will not do it again. You will only get really good dreams, all sweet and innocent. You might say, quite innocent . .

.'

'Have I your permission?' said the Angel to the Ghost.

"I know it will kill my."

'It won't. But suppose it did.

'You're right. It would be more convenient to die than to live with the creature.

'Then I may?'

You're gonna be blasted! You can do it! It's over. You can do whatever you want,' cried the Ghost. But then, he stopped, whining, "God save me." God, help me.

The Ghost gave out a scream that was as intense as anything I have ever heard. The Burning One tightened his grip on the reptile with crimson and then turned it around while it bit and writhed. Finally, he tossed it on the grass, broken backed.

'Ow! The Ghost screamed, "That's it for me," and he stumbled backwards.

I couldn't see anything for a moment. Then, I saw.

between me and the nearest bush, unmistakably solid but growing every moment solider, the upper arm and the shoulder of a man. Then, brighter still and stronger, the legs and hands. The neck and golden head materialised while I watched, and if my attention had not wavered I should have seen the actual completing of a man -- an immense man, naked, not much smaller than the Angel. What distracted me was the fact that at the same moment something seemed to be happening to the Lizard. At first I thought the operation had failed. So far from dying, the creature was still struggling and even growing bigger as it struggled. And as it grew it changed. Its hinder parts grew rounder. The tail, still flickering, became a tail of hair that flickered between huge and glossy buttocks. Suddenly I started back, rubbing my eyes. What stood before me was the greatest stallion I have ever seen, silvery white but with mane and tail of gold. It was smooth and shining, rippled with swells of flesh and muscle, whinneying and stamping with its hoofs. At each stamp the land shook and the trees dindled.

       The new-made man turned and clapped the new horse's neck. It nosed his bright body. Horse and master breathed each into the other's nostrils. The man turned from it, flung himself at the feet of the Burning One, and embraced them. When he rose I thought his face shone with tears, but it may have been only the liquid love and brightness (one cannot distinguish them in that country) which flowed from him. I had not long to think about it. In joyous haste the young man leaped upon the horse's back. Turning in his seat he waved a farewell, then nudged the stallion with his heels. They were off before I knew well what was happening. There was riding if you like! I came out as quickly as I could from among the bushes to follow them with my eyes; but already they were only like a shooting star far off on the green plain, and soon among the foothills of the mountains. Then, still like a star, I saw them winding up, scaling what seemed impossible steeps, and quicker every moment, till near the dim brow of the landscape, so high that I must strain my neck to see them, they vanished, bright themselves, into the rose-brightness of that everlasting morning." (TGD, pp. 350 - 351 - italics in original, underline is mine)

    This man was not "cooperating" or "working with" the grace of God (as synergism teaches). He fought against it. It was the initiative of the Angel that imposed a decision on the part of the man. It was the necessity of a response to the angel that brought about his decision, but he had to decide one way or the other. The man was able to decide to forbear or to give his permission. When he finally acquiesced and gave "permission" there was nothing for him to will in the matter. He surrendered. Gave up. He was knocked back and nearly slain. He did not "work with" the hands of the angel, made crimson by the blood of the savior. It was the work of the self sacrificing Christ on the cross that purchased his redemption. It was the grace of God alone that regenerated him and made him into a new creature." (Note that C. S. Lewis argues against Calvinism when he writes: "Why didn't you kill the damned thing without asking me -- before I knew?").

In *The Voyage Of The Dawn Treader*, C. S. Lewis describes a similar story. Eustace is a regular blighter, always playing the part of Eeyore. Eventually, Eustace is turned into a dragon when he puts on a magical bracelet. He tells the story of how he became a boy again to Edmund:

(Lewis:) "Well, anyway, I looked up and saw the very last thing I expected: a huge lion coming slowly toward me. And one queer thing was that there was no moon last night, but there was moonlight where the lion was. So it came nearer and nearer. I was terribly afraid of it. You may think that, being a dragon, I could have knocked any lion out easily enough. But it wasn't that kind of fear. I wasn't afraid of it eating me, I was just afraid of IT - if you can understand. Well, it came close up to me and looked straight into my eyes. And I shut my eyes tight. But that wasn't any good because it told me to follow it."

"You mean it spoke?"

"I don't know. Now that you mention it, I don't think it did. But it told me all the same. And <u>I knew I'd have to do what it told me</u>, so I got up and followed it. And it led me a long way into the mountains. And there was always this moonlight over and round the lion wherever we went. So at last we came to the top of a mountain I'd never seen before and on the top of this mountain there was a garden -- trees and fruit and everything. In the middle of it there was a well."

"I knew it was a well because you could see the water bubbling up from the bottom of it: but it was a lot bigger than most wells -- like a very big, round bath with marble steps going down into it. The water was as clear as anything and I thought if I could get in there and bathe it would ease the pain in my leg. But the lion told me I must undress first. Mind you, I don't know if he said any words out loud or not."

"I was just going to say that I couldn't undress because I hadn't any clothes on when I suddenly thought that dragons are snaky sort of things and snakes can cast their skins. Oh, of course, thought I, that's what the lion means. So I started scratching myself and my scales began coming off all over the place. And then I scratched a little deeper and, instead of just scales coming off here and there, my whole skin started peeling off beautifully, like it does after an illness, or as if I was a banana. In a minute or two I just stepped out of it. I could see it lying there beside me, looking rather nasty. It was a most lovely feeling. So I started to go down into the well for my bathe."

"But just as I was going to put my feet into the water I looked down and saw that they were all hard and rough and wrinkled and scaly just as they had been before. Oh, that's all right, said I, it only means I had another smaller suit on underneath the first one, and I'll have to get out of it too. So I scratched and tore again and this under-skin peeled off beautifully and out I stepped and left it lying beside the other one and went down to the well for my bathe."

"Well, exactly the same thing happened again. And I thought to myself, oh dear, how ever many skins have I got to take off? For I was longing to bathe my leg. So I scratched away for the third time and got off a third skin, just like the two others, and stepped out of it. But as soon as I looked at myself in the water I knew it had been no good."

"Then the lion said -- but I don't know if it spoke -- <u>You will have to let me undress you</u>.' I was afraid of his claws, I can tell you, but I was pretty nearly desperate now. <u>So I just lay flat down on my back to let him do it</u>."

"The very first tear he made was so deep that I thought it had gone right into my heart. And when he began pulling the skin off, it hurt worse than anything I've ever felt. The only thing that made me able to bear it was

just the pleasure of feeling the stuff peel off. You know -- if you've ever
picked the scab of a sore place. It hurts like billy-oh but it is such fun to see
it coming away."

"I know exactly what you mean," said Edmund.

"Well, <u>he peeled the beastly stuff right off -- just as I thought I'd
done it myself the other three times, only they hadn't hurt</u> -- and there it
was lying on the grass; only ever so much thicker, and darker, and more
knobbly-looking than the others had been. And there was I as smooth and
soft as a peeled switch and smaller than I had been. Then he caught hold of
me -- I didn't like that much for I was very tender underneath now that I'd
no skin on -- and threw me into the water. It smarted like anything but only
for a moment. After that it became perfectly delicious and as soon as I
started swimming and splashing I found that all the pain had gone from my
arm. And then I saw why. I'd turned into a boy again. You'd think me
simply phony if I told you how I felt about my own arms. I know they've no
muscle and are pretty mouldy compared with Caspian's, but I was so glad to
see them."

"After a bit the lion took me out and dressed me --"

"Dressed you. With his paws?"

"Well, I don't exactly remember that bit. But he did somehow or
other: in new clothes -- the same I've got on now, as a matter of fact. And
then suddenly I was back here. Which is what makes me think it must have
been a dream."

"No, it wasn't a dream," said Edmund." (VDT, pp. 473 - 475
underline is mine)

Eustace did not have any choice but to do what Aslan told him to do.
Aslan is portrayed as sovereign and Eustace had to obey and follow him to a
point of decision. Eustace decides to try and do the work himself, to
cooperate with Aslan's instructions. His own attempts to take part in the work
of his salvation failed. It was only after he gave up and did the opposite of
working for his salvation, by choosing to surrender and let Aslan do all the
work that he was saved.

C. S. Lewis explains the process by which he was brought to the point of salvation in *Surprised by Joy*, which is consistent with the previous examples:

(Lewis:) "I felt myself being, there and then, given a free choice. I could open the door or keep it shut; I could unbuckle the armor or keep it on. Neither choice was presented as a duty; no threat or promise was attached to either, though I knew that to open the door or to take off the corslet meant the incalculable. I say, "I chose," yet it did not really seem possible to do the opposite. On the other hand, I was aware of no motives. You could argue that I was not a free agent, but I am more inclined to think that this came nearer to being a perfectly free act than most that I have ever done. <u>Necessity may not be the opposite of freedom</u>, and perhaps a man is most free when, instead of producing motives, he could only say, "I am what I do."

Even if my own philosophy were true, how could the initiative lie on my side? My own analogy, as I now first perceived, suggested the opposite:

 if Shakespeare and Hamlet could ever meet, it must be Shakespeare's doing.

<u>Total surrender, the absolute leap in the dark, were demanded</u>.

You must picture me alone in that room in Magdalen, night after night, feeling, whenever my mind lifted even for a second from my work, the steady, unrelenting approach of Him whom I so earnestly desired not to meet. That which I greatly feared had at last come upon me. In the Trinity Term of 1929 I gave in, and admitted that God was God, and knelt and prayed: perhaps, that night, the most dejected and reluctant convert in all England. I did not then see what is now the most shining and obvious thing; the Divine humility which will accept a convert even on such terms. The prodigal Son at least walked home on his own feet. But who can duly adore that Love which will open the high gates to a prodigal who is brought in kicking, struggling, resentful, and darting his eyes in every direction for a chance of escape? The words *compelle intrare*, compel them to come in, have been so abused by wicked men that we shudder at them; but, properly understood, they plumb the depth of the Divine mercy. The hardness of God is kinder than the softness of men, and His compulsion is our liberation." (SBJ, pp. 123 - 125 - underline is mine, Abridged)

If you need a reminder of who teaches that God "compels them to come in", take a look back at the previous chapter.

Classical Theists believe in inclusivism: that God will hold each person responsible for the amount of revelation that each person received. Every person has the ability to reason his way to God and put his faith in God based on the revelation God has clearly shown to each person in His creation. I believe this is the overall thrust of the book "Miracles" by C. S. Lewis. We are able to "reason" our way to God. If we are not able to reason our way to God, then God is unreasonable. Knowing and believing are two different matters, which is why reason is not sufficient by itself, we must couple reason with experience and 'taste and see that the Lord is good! Blessed is the man who takes refuge in Him!' Psalms 34:8 (Miracles, Ch. 11)

C. S. Lewis describes inclusivism using the perspective of the Calormene soldier in *The Last Battle*. Emeth, which is Hebrew for faithful or true, has served Tash his whole life and cursed Aslan, only to meet Aslan at the end of the world:

(Lewis:) "Then I fell at his feet and thought, Surely this is the hour of death, for the Lion (who is worthy of all honour) will know that I have served Tash all my days and not him. Nevertheless, it is better to see the Lion and die than to be Tisroc of the world and live and not to have seen him. But the Glorious One bent down his golden head and touched my forehead with his tongue and said, 'Son, thou art welcome.' But I said, 'Alas, Lord, I am no son of thine but the servant of Tash.' He answered, 'Child, all the service thou hast done to Tash, I account as service done to me.' Then by reason of my great desire for wisdom and understanding, I overcame my fear and questioned the Glorious One and said, 'Lord, is it then true, as the Ape said, that thou and Tash are one?' The Lion growled so that the earth shook (but his wrath was not against me) and said, 'It is false. Not because he and I are one, but because we are opposites -- I take to me the services which thou hast done to him. For I and he are of such different kinds that no service which is vile can be done to me, and none which is not vile can be done to him. Therefore, if any man swear by Tash and keep his oath for the oath's sake, it is by me that he has truly sworn, though he know it not, and it is I who reward him. And if any man do a cruelty in my name, then, though he says the name Aslan, it is Tash whom he serves and by Tash his deed is accepted. Dost thou understand, Child?' I said, 'Lord, thou knowest how much I understand.' But I said also (for the truth constrained me), 'Yet I have been seeking Tash all my days.' 'Beloved,' said the Glorious One, 'unless thy desire had been for me thou wouldst not have sought so long and so truly.

For all find what they truly seek'."   (TLB, pp. 756 - 757)

=

CHAPTER NINE

~

"For those whom he foreknew he also predestined to be conformed to the image of his Son, in order that he might be the firstborn among many brothers." Romans 8:29 (ESV)

&

"Peter, an apostle of Jesus Christ, To those who are elect exiles of the dispersion in Pontus, Galatia, Cappadocia, Asia, and Bithynia, according to the foreknowledge of God the Father, in the sanctification of the Spirit, for obedience to Jesus Christ and for sprinkling with his blood: May grace and peace be multiplied to you." 1 Peter 1:1 - 2 (ESV)

The view of "election" or "predestination" is derived from which view of total depravity is used. I will begin with the Calvinist view on election. The London Baptist Confession of Faith (1689) explains that predetermination is done independent of foreknowledge:

"God's decree is not based upon His foreknowledge that, under certain conditions, certain happenings will take place, but is independent of all such foreknowledge."

As far as Calvin was concerned, there were only two kinds of election. The first kind of election is done independent of foreknowledge: God determines what will happen, makes His will happen, and knows it will happen. The second kind of election is done dependent on what God foresees will happen:

(Calvin:) "Wherefore, if faith be the fruit of Divine election, it is at once evident that *all* are not enlightened unto faith. Hence, <u>it is also an</u>

indubitable fact, that those on whom God determined in Himself to bestow faith, were chosen of Him from everlasting, for that end. Consequently the sentiments of Augustine are truth, where he thus writes: "The elect of God are chosen by Him to be His children, in order that they *might be made* to believe, not because He foresaw that they *would* believe." (EPG, p. 145 underline is mine - italics in original)

(Boettner:) "The Reformed Faith has held to the existence of an eternal, divine decree which, antecedently to any difference or desert in men themselves separates the human race into two portions and ordains one to everlasting life and the other to everlasting death." (Lorraine Boettner, *The Reformed Doctrine of Predestination*, pp. 83 - 84)

(Storms:) "Rather, election finds its sole and all-sufficient cause in the sovereign good pleasure and grace of God. Were election to be based upon what God foreknows that each individual will do with the gospel it would be an empty and altogether futile act. For what does God foresee in us, apart from His grace? He sees only corruption, ill will, and a pervasive depravity of heart and soul that serves only to evoke His displeasure and wrath." (C. Samuel Storms, *Chosen for Life: An Introductory Guide to the Doctrine of Divine Election*, (Baker Book House, 1987) pp. 29 - 30)

(Five Points:) "God's choice of certain individuals unto salvation before the foundation of the world rested solely in His own sovereign will. His choice of particular sinners was not based on any foreseen response or obedience on their part, such as faith, repentance, etc. On the contrary, God gives faith and repentance to each individual whom He selected. These acts are the result, not the cause of God's choice. Election therefore was not determined by or conditioned upon any virtuous quality or act foreseen in man. Those whom God sovereignly elected He brings through the power of the Spirit to a willing acceptance of Christ. Thus God's choice of the sinner, not the sinner's choice of Christ, is the ultimate cause of salvation." (Five Points, pp. 16 - 17)

The Calvinist view of election is that God's decree determines what He foreknows. God determines everything that will happen, then God foreknows what will happen in the future since He knows what He has determined to take place. The Calvinist view of "total depravity" requires that this election has nothing to do with any goodness in man.

Man is incapable of any spiritual good prior to regeneration, man is "able to do nothing but sin"; Therefore, there can be nothing in man that would cause God to choose any particular man apart from His good pleasure.

It is often pointed out that this belief leads to the logical conclusion that the image of God that man was created with has been "erased". Calvinists call this "utter depravity", and argue that they believe in "total depravity", not "utter depravity". In the previous chapters, I explained how voluntarism leads to the belief that we do not have the ability to know what good is, and the doctrine of total depravity leads to the belief that we are incapable of doing any spiritual good, which includes knowing what good is. This view is not only contradicted by scripture (Genesis 3:22 and Romans 1:20) it is also contradicted by the Natural Law which explains why there is an "ought" which man knows to do. (See book one of *Mere Christianity* and *The Abolition of Man*). Calvin begrudgingly admits to the Natural Law while explaining how the grace of God is universal:

(Calvin:) "That God indeed favours none but the elect alone with the Spirit of regeneration, and that by this they are distinguished from the reprobate; for they are renewed after His image and receive the earnest of the Spirit in hope of the future inheritance, and by the same Spirit the Gospel is sealed in their hearts. But I cannot admit that all this is any reason why He should not grant the reprobate also some taste of His grace, why He should not irradiate their minds with some sparks of His light, why He should not give them some perception of His goodness, and in some sort engrave His word on their hearts." (Commentary on Hebrews Six)

The view of election and predestination that Calvin argues against is that "election is based upon foreknowledge". This is called the "Arminian" view and the following is a description of the Arminian view by a Calvinist:

(Five Points:) (Arminians believe that) "God's choice of certain individuals unto salvation before the foundation of the world was based upon His foreseeing that they would respond to His call. He selected only those whom He knew would of themselves freely believe the gospel. Election therefore was determined by or conditioned upon what man would do. The faith which God foresaw and upon which He based His choice was not given to the sinner by God -- it was not created by the regenerating power of the Holy Spirit -- but resulted solely from man's will. It was left entirely up to man as to who would believe and therefore as to who would be elected unto salvation. God chose those whom He knew would, of their own free will, choose Christ. Thus the sinner's choice of Christ, not God's choice of the sinner, is the ultimate cause of salvation." (Five Points, pp. 16 17 - underline is mine, words in parentheses added for clarification)

In this view God's foreknowledge determines what He decrees: God knows what is going to take place in the future and determines to elect particular individuals based upon this knowledge. Failing to see any other option when it comes to the relationship between determination and foreknowledge sets up a false dichotomy, where we are only allowed to choose between two wrong answers. I have lost track of how many times I have heard someone explain that they cannot understand how their view is correct, but the opposite view is definitely wrong, so their view must be right. For example, "I cannot explain how man is responsible in the Calvinistic view, but the Arminian view leaves salvation completely up to man, so the Calvinist view must be correct". Or, "I cannot explain how man choosing whether or not to believe allows God to remain sovereign over all things, but the Calvinistic view means God is not very loving, so the Arminian view must be correct".

It is a logical fallacy of a false dichotomy to believe that there are only two possibilities when it comes to election and predetermination: "The elect of God are chosen by Him to be His children, in order that they might be made to believe, not because He foresaw that they would believe."

There is a third alternative to predetermination being "independent of" or "based on" foreknowledge. Election may be according to foreknowledge. The best illustration of this is the example of Jesus voluntarily going to the cross, yet Jesus is "the Lamb slain from the foundation of the world" (Revelation 13:8 - ESV). The logical progression looks like this:

1. God knows all things.

2. God knew from eternity that Jesus would die on the cross (Acts 2:23, Rev13:8).

3.   Thus, Jesus must die on the cross. If He had not died on the cross, thenGod would have been wrong in what He foreknew.

4.   Jesus freely chose to die on the cross (John 10:17 - 18).

5.   Therefore, one and the same event is both predetermined and freely chosenat the same time. (See CBF, p. 43)

This view teaches that determination and foreknowledge "are coordinate
acts in the simple and eternal Being of God. Thus, neither determines the other. Rather, God knowingly determined and determinately knew and willed from all eternity everything that would come to pass." (CBF, p. 257) Just as Jesus voluntarily laid down His life and His sacrifice was consistent with "the determinate counsel and foreknowledge of God" (Acts 2:23) from the foundation of the world. It is also logically possible for man to voluntarily surrender his life to God and have this surrender be consistent with election done from the foundation of the world, before any man had done any good or evil:

(Geisler:) "For if God is an eternal and simple Being, then His thoughts must be eternally coordinate and unified. Whatever God forechooses cannot be based on what He foreknows. Nor can what He foreknows be based on what He *forechose*. Both must be simultaneous, eternal, and coordinate acts of God. Thus, our moral actions are truly free, and God determined that they would be such. God is totally sovereign in the sense of actually determining what occurs, and yet man is completely free and responsible for what he chooses." (CBF, p. 53 - italics in original, Abridged)

This view is extensively explained by Geisler in *Chosen But Free*, and in his volumes on systematic theology. C. S. Lewis uses a different explanation than Geisler but arrives at the same conclusions. His position is found in *Miracles*, Appendix B, "On 'Special Providences'". I will not try and summarize or give the highlights of this appendix. I believe you should read it for yourself. This chapter is only intended to give an overview of the three views and to show that which view of election you agree with will be determined by the view of the depravity of man you begin with.

I believe that it will be helpful to look at Ephesians 2:8 - 9 from the perspective of each view of election:

"For by grace you have been saved through faith. And this is not
  your own doing; it is the gift of God, not a result of works, so that no one
  may boast." Ephesians 2:8 - 9 (ESV)

Calvinism: Coercive Monergism: For by grace you have been given the gift of salvation by the gratuitous gift of the ability to believe (faith). And grace, salvation, and faith are not your own doing; grace, salvation, and faith (the ability to believe since man has the total inability to believe) are the gift of God; grace, salvation, and faith (the ability to believe) are given to man not as a result of works, so that no one may boast.

Arminian: Synergism: For by grace you have been given salvation based upon your faith (believing). And salvation is not your own doing alone; salvation is the gift of God, not a result of works but rather a result of working together with God, so that no one may boast.

C. S. Lewis: Persuasive Monergism: For by grace you have been given salvation permitted and received by faith (faith is believing / trusting), And the gift of salvation (eternal life), given by grace, received through faith is not your own doing, salvation by grace through faith is the gift of God, voluntarily surrendering (believing / faith) is not a work, so that no one may boast.

=

CHAPTER TEN

~

"Indeed, under the law almost everything is purified with blood,
  and without the shedding of blood there is no forgiveness of sins."
  Hebrews
  9:22 (ESV)

Son of Man. Lamb of God. Messiah. Great High Priest. Son of God. Each of these names gives us another insight into the nature of Jesus. We gain an additional truth from each of these names. While each is correct in and of itself, the addition of each name adds up to a more complete understanding of Jesus. This is how I view the theories of the atonement. There is no one theory that completely and fully encompasses all aspects of the atonement.

Instead, every valid theory of the atonement adds a new perspective and gives a more complete understanding of the work of Jesus:

(Lewis:) "Now before I became a Christian I was under the impression that the first thing Christians had to believe was one particular theory as to what the point of this dying was. According to that theory God wanted to punish men for having deserted and joined the Great Rebel, but Christ volunteered to be punished instead, and so God let us off. Now I admit that even this theory does not seem to me quite so immoral and so silly as it used to; but that is not the point I want to make. What I came to see later on was that neither this theory nor any other is Christianity. The central Christian belief is that Christ's death has somehow put us right with God and given us a fresh start. Theories as to how it did this are another matter. A good many different theories have been held as to how it works; what all Christians are agreed on is that it does work. I will tell you what I think it is like. All sensible people know that if you are tired and hungry a meal will do you good. But the modern theory of nourishment--all about the vitamins and proteins--is a different thing. People ate their dinners and felt better long before the theory of vitamins was ever heard of: and if the theory of vitamins is some day abandoned they will go on eating their dinners just the same. Theories about Christ's death are not Christianity: they are explanations about how it works. Christians would not all agree as to how important those theories are. My own church--the Church of England--does not lay down any one of them as the right one. the Church of Rome goes a bit further. But I think they will all agree that the thing itself is infinitely more important than any explanations that theologians have produced. I think they would probably admit that no explanation will ever be adequate to reality." (MC, p. 37)

The following is a summary of some of the various views, the main proponent of the view, and what I believe each adds to a more complete understanding of the atonement.

RECAPITULATION THEORY

(Irenaeus:) "God recapitulated in Himself the ancient formation of man, that He might kill sin, deprive death of its power, and vivify man." (*Against Heresies*). Jesus was the second Adam, who lived the perfect life -

overcoming all temptations, kept and fulfilled the law, suffered and died for us, to bring us life.

The ancient formation of man was repeated when Jesus was made flesh:

"Therefore <u>He had to be made like his brothers in every respect</u>, so that he might become a merciful and faithful high priest in the service of God, to make propitiation for the sins of the people. For because He Himself has suffered when tempted, He is able to help those who are being tempted." Hebrews 2:17 - 18 (ESV - underline is mine) The destruction of sin:

"He is the propitiation for our sins, and not for ours only but also for the sins of the whole world." 1 John 2:2 (ESV)

Jesus lived the perfect life and is the perfect sacrifice:

"For we do not have a high priest who is unable to sympathize with our weaknesses, but <u>one who in every respect has been tempted as we are, yet without sin</u>." Hebrews 4:15 (ESV - underline is mine)

"Do not think that I have come to abolish the Law or the Prophets; I have not come to abolish them but to fulfill them. For truly, I say to you, until heaven and earth pass away, not an iota, not a dot, will pass from the Law until all is accomplished." Matthew 5:17 - 18 (ESV)

"For it was indeed fitting that we should have such a high priest, holy, innocent, unstained, separated from sinners, and exalted above the heavens. He has no need, like those high priests, to offer sacrifices daily, first for His own sins and then for those of the people, since He did this once for all when He offered up Himself." Hebrews 7:26 - 27 (ESV) The vivification of man through Jesus:

"For as in Adam all die, so also in Christ shall all be made alive." 1 Corinthians 15:22 (ESV)

"Jesus said to him, "I am the way, and the truth, and the life. No one comes to the Father except through me"." John 14:6 (ESV)

THE RANSOM THEORY

Origen and Augustine. A ransom had to be paid, a penalty or price was demanded and necessary. This price, the blood of Christ, was paid to both Satan and God. Satan received the payment of being able to butcher the perfect lamb. The perfect sacrifice of Christ satisfied the wrath of God, as well as His attribute of justice.

"For even the Son of Man came not to be served but to serve, and to give His life as a ransom for many." Mark 10:45 (ESV)

"And if you call on him as Father who judges impartially according to each one's deeds, conduct yourselves with fear throughout the time of your exile, knowing that you were ransomed from the futile ways inherited from your forefathers, not with perishable things such as silver or gold, but with the precious blood of Christ, like that of a lamb without blemish or spot." 1 Peter 1:17 - 19 (ESV - underline is mine)

MORAL-EXAMPLE THEORY

Pelagius. The example of obedience and trust in the Father by Christ, as well as the sacrifice of Christ for man should inspire the same obedience, trust, and sacrifice in us.

"For to this you have been called, because Christ also suffered for you, leaving you an example, so that you might follow in His steps." 1 Peter 2:21 (ESV)

"Whoever says "I know Him" but does not keep His commandments is a liar, and the truth is not in him, but whoever keeps His word, in him truly the love of God is perfected. By this we may know that we are in Him: whoever says he abides in Him ought to walk in the same way in which He walked." 1 John 2:4 - 6 (ESV)

"You therefore must be perfect, as your heavenly Father is perfect." Matthew 5:48 (ESV)

CHRIST AS VICTOR

Aulen. There is a spiritual war going on between God and Satan. The cross was the victory over death and leads to the final triumph of God over Satan.

"For this perishable body must put on the imperishable, and this mortal body must put on immortality. When the perishable puts on the imperishable, and the mortal puts on immortality, then shall come to pass the saying that is written: "<u>Death is swallowed up in victory</u>." "O death, where is your victory? O death, where is your sting?" The sting of death is sin, and the power of sin is the law. But thanks be to God, <u>who gives us the victory through our Lord Jesus Christ</u>." 1 Corinthians 15:53 - 57 (ESV - underline is mine)

"This was to fulfill what was spoken by the prophet Isaiah: "Behold, my servant whom I have chosen, my beloved with whom my soul is well pleased. I will put my Spirit upon him, and he will proclaim justice to the Gentiles. He will not quarrel or cry aloud, nor will anyone hear his voice in the streets; a bruised reed he will not break, and a smoldering wick he will not quench, <u>until he brings justice to victory</u>; and in his name the Gentiles will hope." Matthew 12 :17 - 20 (ESV - underline is mine)

"Behold my servant, whom I uphold, my chosen, in whom my soul delights; I have put my Spirit upon him; he will bring forth justice to the nations. He will not cry aloud or lift up his voice, or make it heard in the street; a bruised reed he will not break, and a faintly burning wick he will not quench; <u>he will faithfully bring forth justice</u>. He will not grow faint or be discouraged till he has established justice in the earth; and the coastlands wait for his law. Thus says God, the LORD, who created the heavens and stretched them out, who spread out the earth and what comes from it, who gives breath to the people on it and spirit to those who walk in it: "I am the LORD; I have called you in righteousness; I will take you by the hand and keep you; I will give you as a covenant for the people, a light for the nations, to open the eyes that are blind, to bring out the prisoners from the dungeon, from the prison those who sit in darkness. I am the LORD; that is my name; my glory I give to no other, nor my praise to carved idols. Behold, the former things have come to pass, and new things I now declare; before they spring forth I tell you of them." Isaiah 42:1 - 9 (ESV - underline is mine)

"Everyone who believes that Jesus is the Christ has been born of God, and everyone who loves the Father loves whoever has been born of Him. By this we know that we love the children of God, when we love God and obey His commandments. For this is the love of God, that we keep His commandments. And His commandments are not burdensome. For everyone who has been born of God overcomes the world. <u>And this is the victory that has overcome the world--our faith</u>. Who is it that overcomes the world except the one who believes that Jesus is the Son of God?" 1 John 5:1 - 5 (ESV - underline is mine)

NECESSARY-SATISFACTION THEORY

Anselm. It was necessary for Christ to pay the penalty for our sins to satisfy the justice and honor of God which requires either satisfaction, or punishment of the offender:

"He is the propitiation for our sins, and not for ours only but also
    for the sins of the whole world." 1 John 2:2 (ESV)

"For I delivered to you as of first importance what I also
received: that Christ died for our sins in accordance with the Scriptures." 1 Corinthians 15:3 (ESV)

"Grace to you and peace from God our Father and the Lord Jesus Christ, who gave Himself for our sins to deliver us from the present evil age, according to the will of our God and Father, to whom be the glory forever and ever. Amen." Galatians 1:3 - 5 (ESV)

"In this is love, not that we have loved God but that he loved us
and sent his Son to be the propitiation for our sins." 1 John 4:10 (ESV)

"And being made perfect, He became the source of eternal
salvation to all who obey him, being designated by God a high priest after the order of Melchizedek." Hebrews 5:9 - 10 (ESV)

"But when Christ appeared as a high priest of the good things that have come, then through the greater and more perfect tent (not made with hands, that is, not of this creation) He entered once for all into the holy places, not by means of the blood of goats and calves but <u>by means of His own blood, thus securing an eternal redemption</u>. For if the blood of goats and bulls, and the sprinkling of defiled persons with the ashes of a heifer, sanctify for the purification of the flesh, how much more will the blood of Christ, who through the eternal Spirit offered Himself without blemish to

God, purify our conscience from dead works to serve the living God."
Hebrews 9:11 - 14 (ESV - underline is mine)

"He has appeared once for all at the end of the ages
to put away
sin by the sacrifice of Himself. And just as it is appointed for man to die
once, and after that comes judgment, so Christ, having been offered once to
bear the sins of many, will appear a second time, not to deal with sin but to
save those who are eagerly waiting for Him." Hebrews 9:26b - 28 (ESV)

"But when Christ had offered for all time a single
sacrifice for
sins, He sat down at the right hand of God, waiting from that time until His
enemies should be made a footstool for His feet. For by a single offering He
has perfected for all time those who are being sanctified." Hebrews 10:12 -
14 (ESV)

"For the wages of sin is death, but the free gift of
God is eternal
life in Christ Jesus our Lord." Romans 6:23 (ESV)

"Truly, truly, I say to you, whoever hears my word
and believes
Him who sent me has eternal life. He does not come into judgment, but has
passed from death to life." John 5:24 (ESV)

Jesus is the source of eternal life which He purchased by His own blood.
It is the gift of eternal life that He freely gives to all who believe in Him.

(Geisler:) "The salvation of everyone was not immediately *applied*;
it was simply *purchased*. All persons were *made savable*, but not all persons
were *automatically saved*. The gift was made possible by the Saviour, but it
must be received by the sinner. In short, the salvation of all sinners from
God's eternal wrath is possible, but only those who accept Christ's payment
for their sins will actually be saved from it." (ST 2, p. 405 - italics in
original)

When I go to the store and purchase a new coat, I pay for the coat with
cash; However, I earned the cash by trading some of my time, talents, and
health to earn the cash. While it is common to say "I paid cash for it", what is
really meant is that "I used part of my life to get the cash to buy the coat."

This is similar to the atonement. Jesus gave his time, talents, and life to satisfy the wrath of God and force Satan to relinquish the rightful claim of ownership he has on our lives because of our sin. It is with His own blood that Jesus purchases eternal life and the ability to be redeemed (to be bought back). It is the gift of eternal life that He offers to everyone. This gift is received by faith (believing).

> "You are not your own, for you were bought with a price. So glorify God in your body." 1 Corinthians 6:19b - 20 (ESV)

"But false prophets also arose among the people, just as there will be false teachers among you, who will secretly bring in destructive heresies, even denying the Master who bought them, bringing upon themselves swift destruction." 2 Peter 2:1 (ESV)

Just as I could say that I bought my new coat with my time, talents, and health; skipping over the step of using the cash I received from my work to purchase the coat: I can also say that I have been bought with the blood of Jesus, skipping over the step of eternal life.

The Atonement was universal. The scriptures say that "all", "everyone", and "the sins of the whole world" were paid for by the sacrifice of Jesus. Apostasy is denying the one who bought you. This means that everyone has been bought with the price of the blood of Jesus, and everyone that rejects Him is Apostate. You do not have to be a believer to "apostatize" and deny The One who bought you; Instead, you are an unbeliever and apostate: denying The One who bought you.

This is how I understand the Necessary Satisfaction view of the atonement: Jesus atoned for everyone in particular, and for the sins of everyone, satisfying the wrath of God. He purchased the gift of eternal life (Rom 6:23). This is the gift that is offered to all and given upon belief (faith). The following are the individual components of the Atonement which are supported by the various views discussed above:

Universal & Particular--Jesus died for every person:

> "He is the propitiation for our sins, and not for ours only but also for the sins of the whole world." 1 John 2:2 (ESV)

"But we see him who for a little while was made lower than the angels, namely Jesus, crowned with glory and honor because of the suffering of death, so that by the grace of God He might taste death for everyone."
Hebrews 2:9 (ESV)

"For there is one God, and there is one mediator between God and men, the man Christ Jesus, who gave Himself as a ransom for all, which is the testimony given at the proper time." 1 Timothy 2:5 - 6 (ESV)

(Lewis:) "It is an old and pious saying that Christ died not only for Man but for each man, just as much as if each had been the only man there was." (LTM, p. 55)

Voluntary--Jesus chose to die for everyone:

"For this reason the Father loves me, because I lay down my life that I may take it up again. No one takes it from me, but I lay it down of my own accord. I have authority to lay it down, and I have authority to take it up again. This charge I have received from my Father." John 10:17 - 18 (ESV)

Necessary--Without the atonement, fallen man could not be redeemed and saved:

"Indeed, under the law almost everything is purified with blood, and without the shedding of blood there is no forgiveness of sins. Thus it was necessary for the copies of the heavenly things to be purified with these rites, but the heavenly things themselves with better sacrifices than these.

For Christ has entered, not into holy places made with hands, which are copies of the true things, but into heaven itself, now to appear in the presence of God on our behalf." Hebrews 9:22 - 24 (ESV)

Penal--The punishment for our sins was satisfied in the suffering of our Saviour. Jesus paid the price for us:

"But he was wounded for our transgressions; he was crushed for our iniquities; upon him was the chastisement that brought us peace, and with his stripes we are healed. All we like sheep have gone astray; we have turned--every one--to his own way; and the LORD has laid on him the iniquity of us all." Isaiah 53:5 - 6 (ESV)

Perfect--Jesus was the perfect man and made the perfect sacrifice:

"And being made perfect, He became the source of eternal salvation to all who obey him, being designated by God a high priest after the order of Melchizedek." Hebrews 5:9 - 10 (ESV)

"But with the precious blood of Christ, like that of a lamb without blemish or spot." 1 Peter 1:19 (ESV)

"For we do not have a high priest who is unable to sympathize with our weaknesses, but one who in every respect has been tempted as we are, yet without sin." Hebrews 4:15 (ESV)

"How much more will the blood of Christ, who through the eternal Spirit offered Himself without blemish to God, purify our conscience from dead works to serve the living God." Hebrews 9:14 (ESV)

Substitutionary--Christ died for our sins and for us!:

"For while we were still weak, at the right time Christ died for the ungodly. For one will scarcely die for a righteous person--though perhaps for a good person one would dare even to die-- but God shows his love for us in that while we were still sinners, Christ died for us." Romans 5:6 - 8 (ESV)

"He Himself bore our sins in His body on the tree, that we might die to sin and live to righteousness. By His wounds you have been healed." 1 Peter 2:24 (ESV)

"For Christ also suffered once for sins, the righteous for the unrighteous, that He might bring us to God, being put to death in the flesh but made alive in the spirit." 1 Peter 3:18 (ESV)

While scripture does not literally say that Jesus "died in our place", the story of Abraham and Isaac allows for the perspective and insight that Jesus, the Lamb of God, died in our place:

"Abraham said, "God will provide for himself the lamb for a
burnt offering, my son." So they went both of them together. When they came to the place of which God had told him, Abraham built the altar there and laid the wood in order and bound Isaac his son and laid him on the altar, on top of the wood. Then Abraham reached out his hand and took the knife to slaughter his son. But the angel of the LORD called to him from heaven and said, "Abraham, Abraham!" And he said, "Here am I." He said, "Do not lay your hand on the boy or do anything to him, for now I know that you fear God, seeing you have not withheld your son, your only son, from me." And Abraham lifted up his eyes and looked, and behold, behind him was a ram, caught in a thicket by his horns. And Abraham went and took the ram and offered it up as a burnt offering instead of his son. So Abraham called the name of that place, "The LORD will provide"; as it is said to this day, "On the mount of the LORD it shall be provided." Genesis 22:8 - 14 (ESV)

Additionally, in *The Lion, The Witch, and The* Wardrobe, C. S. Lewis has Aslan die in the place of Edmund. This is certainly a beautiful picture of the suffering and sacrifice of Christ in our place and on our behalf because He loves us; However, Aslan did not die in the place of Peter, Lucy, or Susan. We can stretch the meaning of the substitutionary aspect of the atonement beyond its intent by saying that Jesus died in the place of every person. Yet, he certainly did die to defeat the witch, purchase salvation, and save Peter, Lucy, and Susan. The substitutionary atonement gives us an incredible insight into the worth that God places on each one of us: That Jesus would have died to save any one of us, and in fact He would have died just to save one of us. It is not the number saved that compelled Him to sacrifice Himself, but His love for us.

"Anyone who does not love does not know God, because God is
love. In this the love of God was made manifest among us, that God sent his only Son into the world, so that we might live through Him. In this is love, not that we have loved God but that He loved us and sent His Son to

be the propitiation for our sins. Beloved, if God so loved us, we also ought to love one another." 1 John 4:8 - 11 (ESV)

(Lewis:) "We were made not primarily that we may love God (though we were made for that too) but that God may love us, that we may become objects in which the Divine love may rest 'well pleased'." (POP, p. 388)

The atonement is Universal, Particular, Voluntary, Necessary, Penal, Perfect, Substitutionary, and Good News! C. S. Lewis brings many of the various elements and views of the atonement together in the following:

(Lewis:) "But supposing God became a man--suppose our human nature which can suffer and die was amalgamated with God's nature in one person--then that person could help us. He could surrender His will, and suffer and die, because He was man; and He could do it perfectly because He was God. You and I can go through this process only if God does it in us; but God can do it only if He becomes man. Our attempts at this dying will succeed only if we men share in God's dying, just as our thinking can succeed only because it is a drop out of the ocean of His intelligence: but we cannot share God's dying unless God dies; and He cannot die except by being a man. That is the sense in which He pays our debt, and suffers for us what He Himself need not suffer at all." (MC, p. 39)

(Lewis:) "The perfect submission, the perfect suffering, the
perfect death were not only easier to Jesus because He was God, but were possible only because He was God." (MC, p. 39)

=

CHAPTER ELEVEN

~

"I suppose there are two views about everything"
"Eh? Two views? There are a dozen views about everything until you know the answer. Then there's never more than one."
(C. S. Lewis, *That Hideous Strength*, p. 70) -------------------

-

Foundation of Reformed Theology / Calvinism:

1. God is free to over-rule any of His creatures' decisions.

2. A. God is OmniscientB. God is Omnipotent

       C.   God is Perfect

3. A. God knew the fall would happen.B.

       C.   God did not need to create anything.

---

3.   B. God could have stopped the fall from happening.

4.   The fall was willed, ordained, and decreed by God > Everything thathappens is the will of God.

5.   No free-will in man or angel.

6.   Correct because God wills it. > Created for the Glory of God.

7.   Man does not know what good is.

8.   Total Depravity or Total Inability. > Three meanings of Faith.

9.   Unconditional Election. > Predetermination independent of Foreknowledge.

10.   Limited Atonement. > God able to save all - will save all that Jesus diedfor.

11.   Irresistible Effectual Grace > Grace universal

---

12.   Perseverance of the Saints. > Those that "fall from the faith" were neversaved.

Each belief in the system of Calvinism or Reformed Theology is like a brick in a stack. Each brick, or belief, is laid upon the brick that comes before it. Each brick inexorably leads to the selection of the next brick. If the belief held in any one of the bricks that are in-between the solid lines is incorrect, not only does that brick fall, but the belief that led to that brick, and the brick that is about to be built upon that belief also falls. This is why it is called "Systematic Theology," everything is interconnected.

Unfortunately, the failure by Augustine, Luther, Calvin, and Sproul to see that their view of the attribute of the Omnipotence of God was based on a logical contradiction has led them to believe in a system of error that is known today as Calvinism.

(Lewis:) "If you have taken a wrong turning, then to go forward
 does not get you any nearer. If you are on the wrong road, progress means doing an about-turn and walking back to the right road; and in that case the man who turns back soonest is the most progressive man." (MC, p. 23) Turning back to reconsider the attribute of the Omnipotence of God corrects the error made by Calvinists and leads to an entirely different system of belief. While you may not agree that Classical Theists have the correct view of Omnipotence and therefore the correct systematic theology, at least you will know why the views and interpretations of Calvinists differ from the rest of Christianity.

This brings us to a consideration of the pinnacle of both systems of belief: The perseverance of the saints. Eternal security does not topple with the rest of Reformed Theology since it is supported by two areas that both systems agree on: Election and Omniscience. The logical conclusion of both election being predetermined independent of foreknowledge, as well as election being predetermined according to foreknowledge is that God knows for sure who will have faith and put their trust in Him.

Both systems believe that "justification is by faith alone". Calvinism teaches that justification happens when God forces the gift of faith on man. It is this gift of faith that causes justification and regeneration: the forgiveness of sins that brings new life. Justification (the forgiveness of sins) brings regeneration (being born again to a new life) which precedes faith (believing).

C. S. Lewis also teaches that "justification is by faith alone". Faith (believing), is surrendering yourself back to God -- this surrender requires you to stop trying to do it yourself and let God do the work. It is this faith that allows justification which brings regeneration via the gift of salvation or eternal life. The credit for the gift goes to the giver of the gift, not the recipient of the gift. (How many children have you seen walking around after Christmas patting themselves on the back for the great gift they got themselves by being brilliant enough to believe the package under the tree with their name on it was really for them?)

In *Surprised by Joy*, C. S. Lewis gives an account of his conversion. His account is different from the account of Augustines conversion. The process by which God pursues man varies to such an extent that "testimony time" is a popular way for a group of believers to bond together. Both G. K. Chesterton and C. S. Lewis liken this process to fishing:

(Chesterton:) " 'Did you catch this man?' asked the colonel, frowning.

Father Brown looked him full in his frowning face. 'Yes,' he said, 'I caught him, with an unseen hook and an invisible line which is long enough to let him wander to the ends of the world, and still to bring him back with a twitch upon the thread'." (Father Brown, p. 60)

(Lewis:) "And so the great Angler played His fish and I never dreamed that the hook was in my tongue." (SBJ, p. 116)

This is the process by which God draws us to Himself: "Nevertheless, I tell you the truth: it is to your advantage that I go away, for if I do not go away, the Helper will not come to you. But if I go, I will send him to you. And when he comes, he will convict the world concerning sin and righteousness and judgment: concerning sin, because they do not believe in me; concerning righteousness, because I go to the Father, and you will see me no longer; concerning judgment, because the ruler of this world is judged." John 16:7 - 11 (ESV)

The Holy Spirit convicts or convinces everyone of their sin. We do not have a choice when it comes to whether or not we will be convicted by the Holy Spirit. We are compelled to make a decision. This is what C. S. Lewis means when he writes, "Necessity may not be the opposite of freedom". (SBJ, p. 123). When the Holy Spirit compels us to be convinced of sin and righteousness, we do not have any choice whether or not we have to make a choice; However, we do have the ability to choose one way or the other: we can choose to be convicted to righteousness, or to be convicted to judgment:

"Because, if you confess with your mouth that Jesus is Lord and
  believe in your heart that God raised him from the dead, you will be saved.
  For with the heart one believes and is justified, and with the mouth one
  confesses and is saved." Romans 10:9 - 10 (ESV)

The moment we surrender to God, putting our faith and trust in Jesus, we are justified and given the gift of eternal life or salvation. As we just read in Romans 10:10, believing precedes justification. Justification means that God does not count our sins against us:

"That is, in Christ, God was reconciling the world to
    Himself, not
  counting their trespasses against them, and entrusting to us the message of
  reconciliation. Therefore, we are ambassadors for Christ, God making his
  appeal through us. We implore you on behalf of Christ, be reconciled to
  God." 2 Corinthians 5:19 - 20 (ESV)

At the point of believing, we are justified and "put on" the righteousness of Jesus like a robe -- Just as Aslan dressed Eustace. While our sins are forgiven at this point, we are still imperfect and will continue to sin. From the moment of justification on, we will always be viewed through the perfect finished atonement of Jesus. When God looks at us, He sees the righteousness of the Saviour. We cannot be justified or declared righteous a second time since this would require a second crucifixion of the Saviour:

"For it is impossible, in the case of those who have
    once been
  enlightened, who have tasted the heavenly gift, and have shared in the Holy
  Spirit, and have tasted the goodness of the word of God and the powers of
  the age to come, and then have fallen away, to restore them again to
  repentance, since they are crucifying once again the Son of God to their own
  harm and holding him up to contempt." Hebrews 6:4 - 6 (ESV)

From the point of justification on begins the process of sanctification:

"Therefore, my beloved, as you have always obeyed,
    so now, not

only as in my presence but much more in my absence, work out your own salvation with fear and trembling, for it is God who works in you, both to will and to work for His good pleasure." Philippians 2:12 - 13 (ESV)

"But when Christ had offered for all time a single sacrifice for sins, He sat down at the right hand of God, waiting from that time until His enemies should be made a footstool for His feet. For by a single offering he has perfected for all time those who are being sanctified." Hebrews 10:12 - 14 (ESV)

"But now that you have been set free from sin and have become slaves of God, the fruit you get leads to sanctification and its end, eternal life." Romans 6:22 (ESV)

Sanctification is the lifelong process of doing the good works that God has prepared for us to do (see Ephesians 2:10). The amount of joy we experience in this life can be measured in direct proportion to our obedience to God and doing His will for us. The commandments to live a righteous life apart from the pollution of the world are not burdens. Rather, following Jesus will heap up eternal blessings for ourselves as well as being beneficial to us in our life.

Jesus was crucified from the foundation of the world as well as a point in time. God chose the elect from the foundation of the world, yet the elect are adopted as sons at a point in time. The elect are sealed by the Holy Spirit at the time of justification, yet this sealing is for a future time when we take possession of the inheritance we have been promised. The elect are also considered justified (declared righteous) at a point in time, yet we will experience justification (being made righteous) at a future point in time when we are judged and glorified.

"In Him you also, when you heard the word of truth, the gospel of your salvation, and believed in Him, were sealed with the promised Holy Spirit, who is the guarantee of our inheritance until we acquire possession of it, to the praise of his glory." Ephesians 1:13 - 14 (ESV)

"When the Son of Man comes in his glory, and all the angels with Him, then He will sit on His glorious throne. Before Him will be gathered all the nations, and He will separate people one from another as a shepherd separates the sheep from the goats. And He will place the sheep on His right, but the goats on the left. Then the King will say to those on His right, 'Come, you who are blessed by My Father, inherit the kingdom prepared for you from the foundation of the world'.

Then He will say to those on His left, 'Depart from me, you cursed, into the eternal fire prepared for the devil and his angels'." Matthew 25:31 34, 41 (ESV)

"Then I saw a great white throne and Him who was seated on it. From His presence earth and sky fled away, and no place was found for them. And I saw the dead, great and small, standing before the throne, and books were opened. Then another book was opened, which is the book of life. And the dead were judged by what was written in the books, according to what they had done. And the sea gave up the dead who were in it, Death and Hades gave up the dead who were in them, and they were judged, each one of them, according to what they had done. Then Death and Hades were thrown into the lake of fire. This is the second death, the lake of fire. And if anyone's name was not found written in the book of life, he was thrown into the lake of fire." Revelation 20:11 - 15 (ESV)

Process, Point, Process, Point: Salvation is a <u>process</u> by which God draws us to Him through circumstances and the conviction of the Holy Spirit. Then there is a <u>point</u> in time at which we believe and are justified and sealed by the Holy Spirit. We work out our salvation in the <u>process</u> of sanctification until we reach the final <u>point</u> of judgment and vindication by the blood of the Lamb along with receipt of a glorified body and participation in the kingdom of God.

The question of 'perseverance of the saints', or 'once saved always saved' still remains. Calvin notes that the perseverance of the saints is underpinned by election (and election is grounded in foreknowledge or omniscience: See Ephesians 1):

(Calvin:) "When Christ declares that He will by no means cast out one of those who do come unto Him; nay, that the life of all such is hidden and kept in security, in Himself, until He shall raise them up at the last day; who does not see here that <u>the final perseverance of the saints </u>(as it is commonly termed) is in like manner <u>ascribed to the election of God</u>? It may be, and has been, that <u>some fall from the faith</u>; but those who are given to Christ by the Father are, as Christ Himself declares, placed beyond the peril of destruction." (EPG, p. 36 - parenthetical note in original, underline is mine)

I understand Calvin to be using the word "faith" in this sentence to mean a system of belief or what we call "religion":

> (Calvin:) "Every tree that my heavenly Father hath not planted,

shall be rooted up." Whereby He plainly intimates, that the reprobate also sometimes take root, in appearance, and yet, are not planted by the hand of God." (EPG, p. 156)

Jesus may be describing those that "fall from the faith" in Matthew 13 as a "tare" or a "weed". These are people that "believe" there is a God, but never surrender or put their trust in Him. Believing in this context is nothing more than an intellectual assent that there is a God. Just as the demons believe there is a God and tremble:

"So also faith by itself, if it does not have works, is dead. But someone will say, "You have faith and I have works." Show me your faith apart from your works, and I will show you my faith by my works. You believe that God is one; you do well. Even <u>the demons believe--and shudder</u>! Do you want to be shown, you foolish person, that faith apart from works is useless? Was not Abraham our father justified by works when he offered up his son Isaac on the altar? You see that faith was active along with his works, and <u>faith was completed by his works</u>; and the Scripture was fulfilled that says, "Abraham believed God, and it was counted to him as righteousness"--and he was called a friend of God. You see that <u>a person is justified by works and not by faith alone</u>." James 2:17 - 24 (ESV - underline is mine)

In *Christian Behavior*, which is book three in *Mere Christianity*, Chapters 11 and 12 are both titled "FAITH". C. S. Lewis does a far better job of explaining the relationship between faith and works in regards to salvation that I could ever hope to. You should read the chapters for yourself, but I will string a few sentences together to give the sense of what he says:

(Lewis:) "We cannot discover our failure to keep God's law except by trying our very hardest (and then failing). All this trying leads up to the vital moment at which you turn to God and say, 'You must do this. I can't.' It is the change from being confident about our own efforts to the state in which we despair of doing anything for ourselves and leave it to God. I know the words 'leave it to God' can be misunderstood, but they must stay for the moment. The sense in which a Christian leaves it to God is that he puts all his trust in Christ: trusts that Christ will somehow share with him the perfect human obedience which He carried out from His birth to His crucifixion: that Christ will make the man more like Himself and, in a sense, make good his deficiencies. And, in yet another sense, handing everything over to Christ does not, of course, mean that you stop trying. To trust Him means, of course, trying to do all that He says. There would be no sense in saying you trusted a person if you would not take his advice. Christians have often disputed as to whether what leads the Christian home is good actions, or Faith in Christ. I have no right really to speak on such a difficult question, but it does seem to me like asking which blade in a pair of scissors is most necessary. A serious moral effort is the only thing that will bring you to the point where you throw up the sponge. Faith in Christ is the only thing to save you from despair at that point: and out of that Faith in Him good actions must inevitably come." (MC, p. 81 - Abridged)

I think it should be clear by this point that it is God who does all the "work" at the point of justification in salvation:

"I give them eternal life, and they will never perish, and no one will snatch them out of my hand. My Father, who has given them to me, is greater than all, and no one is able to snatch them out of the Father's hand. I and the Father are one." John 10:28 - 30 (ESV)

Those that believe that predestination is based upon foreknowledge will be correct in saying that you can take yourself out of the Father's hand and no longer have eternal life. They note that this verse only teaches that no one else is able to snatch you out of the Father's hand. You do not snatch yourself out; Instead, you will your salvation away, and deliberately forfeit eternal life. This is the peril of salvation based on God's foreknowledge of your faith. If it is your faith that puts you in, your confidence in your salvation is only as good as how confident you are in your continued faith. This is why C. S. Lewis and scripture teach that it is believing/faith that accepts the gift of salvation that is given by grace. It was Jesus that did the "work" of atoning for your sins. We do the believing. Jesus does the justifying. He is the one that puts you into His hand and gives you eternal, not temporary, life.

"For which I was appointed a preacher and apostle and teacher, which is why I suffer as I do. But I am not ashamed, for I know whom I have believed, and <u>I am convinced that He is able to guard until that Day what I have entrusted to Him</u>." 2 Timothy 1:11 -12 (ESV - footnote version - underline is mine)

Once again scripture teaches that those who believe and put their trust in the finished work of Christ, have the confidence that their salvation is secure in the hands of Jesus Himself. It is Jesus that is guarding the gift of eternal life that believers have been given. This verse also illustrates the opposing view that Calvinists hold. The following is the same verse in the text in the ESV (which is sometimes referred to as the Reformed Standard Version), rather than the more literal translation found in the footnote of the ESV, and most other versions of the Bible:

"But I am not ashamed, for I know whom I have believed, and I am convinced that he is able to guard until that Day <u>what has been entrusted to me</u>."

This change in the verse supports the Reformed belief in coercive monergism. Instead of putting our trust in Jesus: faith, repentance, justification, and eternal life are given or entrusted to the elect.

"I write these things to you who believe in the name of the Son of God that you may know that you have eternal life." 1 John 5:13 (ESV)

If you believe predestination is based on foreknowledge, you have to put your confidence in your ability to persevere in your faith. If you believe predestination is independent of foreknowledge, you have to hope that the faith you have is actually a gift from God, and not your own attempts to join a religion. If you 'fall away' from the church, or fail to persevere to the end, your former cell mates will simply say that you were never saved, as **R. C.** Sproul explains:

>(Sproul:) "If we have it we never lose it; if we lose it we never had it." (CBG, p. 180)

If you believe that predestination is according to foreknowledge, you put your confidence in Jesus to guard the gift of eternal life He gave you when you put your trust in Him. You put your confidence in the sealing of the Holy Spirit, and the guarantee of your future inheritance. You can actually know right now that you have eternal life:

>(Calvin:) "Believers ought to rest in the certainty of their salvation." (EPG, p. 124)

(Calvin:) "The Holy Spirit, therefore, nowhere exhorts us to the care and exercise of prayer, under any idea, that our salvation fluctuates in a state of uncertainty or doubt: for it rests safely in the hand of God." (EPG, p. 125)

Now that the riddle of the Reformation has been solved, perhaps the Calvinists and Arminians can cease their arguing. Protestants can apologize to Roman Catholics, and Roman Catholics can reconsider salvation by grace through faith - not by works but inevitably with works. Imagine what the Church can accomplish when the saints unite and press on to Orthopraxy:

>"Religion that is pure and undefiled before God, the Father, is this: to visit orphans and widows in their affliction, and to keep oneself unstained from the world." James 1:27 (ESV)

=

APPENDIX ONE: CREEDS

~

THE APOSTLES CREED

~

I believe in God the Father Almighty: Creator of Heaven and earth.

And in Jesus Christ, His only Son, our Lord;

Who was conceived by the Holy Spirit, born of the Virgin Mary,

Suffered under Pontius Pilate, was crucified, dead, and buried;

He descended into hell; on the third day He rose again from the dead;

He ascended into Heaven, where He sits at the right hand of God the Father Almighty;

From thence He shall come to judge the living and the dead.

I believe in the Holy Spirit,

One holy catholic Church,

The communion of the saints,

The forgiveness of sins, The

resurrection of the body,

And life everlasting.

~

THE NICENE CREED

~

We believe in one God, the Father Almighty, maker of heaven and earth, and of all things visible and invisible. And in one Lord Jesus Christ, the only begotten Son of God, and born of the Father before all ages. (God of God) light of light, true God of true God. Begotten not made, consubstantial to the Father, by whom all things were made. Who for us men and for our salvation came down from heaven. And was incarnate of the Holy Spirit and of the Virgin Mary and was made man; was crucified also for us under Pontius Pilate, suffered and was buried; and the third day rose again according to the Scriptures. And ascended into heaven, sits at the right hand of the Father, and shall come again with glory to judge the living and the dead, of whose Kingdom there shall be no end. And (I believe) in the Holy Spirit, the Lord and Giver of life, who proceeds from the Father (and the Son), who together with the Father and the Son is to be adored and glorified, who spoke by the Prophets. And one holy, catholic, and apostolic Church. We confess one baptism for the remission of sins. And we look for the resurrection of the dead and the life of the world to come. Amen.

~

THE ATHANASIAN CREED

~

Whosoever will be saved, before all things it is necessary that he hold the Catholic Faith. Which Faith except everyone do keep whole and undefiled, without doubt he shall perish everlastingly. And the Catholic Faith is this, that we worship one God in Trinity and Trinity in Unity. Neither confounding the Persons, nor dividing the Substance. For there is one Person of the Father, another of the Son, and another of the Holy Spirit. But the Godhead of the Father, of the Son and of the Holy Spirit is all One, the Glory Equal, the
Majesty Co-Eternal. Such as the Father is, such is the Son, and such is the Holy Spirit. The Father Uncreated, the Son Uncreated, and the Holy Spirit Uncreated. The Father Incomprehensible, the Son Incomprehensible, and the Holy Spirit Incomprehensible. The Father Eternal, the Son Eternal, and the Holy Spirit Eternal and yet they are not Three Eternals but One Eternal. As also there are not Three Uncreated, nor Three Incomprehensibles, but One Uncreated, and One Uncomprehensible. So likewise the Father is Almighty, the Son Almighty, and the Holy Spirit Almighty. And yet they are not Three Almighties but One Almighty.

So the Father is God, the Son is God, and the Holy Spirit is God. And yet they are not Three Gods, but One God. So likewise the Father is Lord, the Son Lord, and the Holy Spirit Lord. And yet not Three Lords but One Lord. For, like as we are compelled by the Christian verity to acknowledge every Person by Himself to be God and Lord, so are we forbidden by the Catholic Religion to say, there be Three Gods or Three Lords. The Father is made of none, neither created, nor begotten. The Son is of the Father alone; not made, nor created, but begotten. The Holy Spirit is of the Father, and of the Son neither made, nor created, nor begotten, but proceeding.

So there is One Father, not Three Fathers; one Son, not Three Sons; One Holy Spirit, not Three Holy Spirits. And in this Trinity none is afore or after Other, None is greater or less than Another, but the whole Three Persons are

Co-eternal together, and Co-equal. So that in all things, as is aforesaid, the Unity in Trinity, and the Trinity in Unity, is to be worshipped. He therefore that will be saved, must thus think of the Trinity.

Furthermore, it is necessary to everlasting Salvation, that he also believe rightly the Incarnation of our Lord Jesus Christ. For the right Faith is, that we believe and confess, that our Lord Jesus Christ, the Son of God, is God and Man. God, of the substance of the Father, begotten before the worlds; and Man, of the substance of His mother, born into the world. Perfect God and Perfect Man, of a reasonable Soul and human Flesh subsisting. Equal to the Father as touching His Godhead, and inferior to the Father as touching His Manhood. Who, although He be God and Man, yet He is not two, but One Christ. One, not by conversion of the Godhead into Flesh, but by taking of the Manhood into God. One altogether, not by confusion of substance, but by Unity of Person. For as the reasonable soul and flesh is one Man, so God and Man is one Christ. Who suffered for our salvation, descended into Hell, rose again the third day from the dead. He ascended into Heaven, He sits on the right hand of the Father, God Almighty, from whence He shall come to judge the quick and the dead. At whose coming all men shall rise again with their bodies, and shall give account for their own works. And they that have done good shall go into life everlasting, and they that have done evil into everlasting fire. This is the Catholic Faith, which except a man believe faithfully and firmly, he cannot be saved.

=

APPENDIX TWO: PHILOSOPHY

~

"Come now, let us reason together, says the LORD." Isaiah 1:18

~

Philosophy: The rational investigation of the truths and principles of being, knowledge, or conduct. (Dictionary.com)

~

In short, everyone has a philosophy, whether they have thought it through or not. Our philosophy is the framework through which we look at the world. I like to think of this framework as a set of filters in our mind. When we experience something, we run the experience through this set of filters to reach a conclusion or derive some sort of meaning. C. S. Lewis gives an excellent account of how this works.

(Lewis:) "What we learn from experience depends on the kind of philosophy we bring to experience. It is therefore useless to appeal to experience before we have settled, as well as we can, the philosophical question." (Miracles, p. 211) "The result of our historical enquiries thus depends on the philosophical views which we have been holding before we even began to look at the evidence. This philosophical question must therefore come first." (Miracles, p. 211)

C. S. Lewis gives an example of how we can arrive at a forgone conclusion if we do not examine the philosophical framework we are using to determine the facts:

(Lewis:) "Here is an example of the sort of thing that happens if we omit the preliminary philosophical task, and rush on to the historical. In a popular commentary on the Bible you will find a discussion of the date at which the Fourth Gospel was written. The author says it must have been written after the execution of St. Peter, because, in the Fourth Gospel, Christ is represented as predicting the execution of St. Peter. 'A book', thinks the author, 'cannot be written *before* events which it refers to'. Of course it cannot -- unless real predictions ever occur. If they do, then his argument for the date is in ruins. And the author has not discussed at all whether real predictions are possible. He takes it for granted (perhaps unconsciously) that they are not. Perhaps he is right: but if he is, he has not discovered this principle by historical inquiry. He has brought his disbelief in predictions to his historical work, so to speak, ready made. Unless he had done so his historical conclusion about the date of the Fourth Gospel could not have been reached at all. His work is therefore quite useless to a person who wants to know *whether* predictions occur. The author gets to work only after he has already answered that question in the negative, and on grounds which he never communicates to us." (Miracles, p. 211 - 212)

R.C. Sproul gives an excellent description of the shared philosophy of Calvin and C. S. Lewis. This is the orthodox philosophy about God, and since it is about God, it is tempting to call it theology instead of philosophy.

This philosophy began with Augustine but was systematized by Thomas Aquinas in his *Summa Theologica*:

(Sproul:) "When we consider love as an attribute of God, we recognize that it is defined in relation to all the other attributes of God. This is true not only of love but also of every other attribute of God. It is important to remember that when we speak of the attributes of God, we are speaking of properties that cannot be reduced to composite parts. One of the first affirmations we make about the nature of God is that He is not a composite being. Rather we confess that God is a simple being. This does not mean that God is 'easy' in the sense that a simple task is not a difficult task. Here simplicity is not contrasted with difficulty but with composition. A being who is composite is made up of definite parts. As a human creature, I am composed of many parts, such as arms, legs, eyes, ears, lungs, etc."

(Sproul:) "As a simple being, God is not made up of parts as we are. This is crucial to any proper understanding of the nature of God. This means that God is not partly immutable, partly omniscient, partly omnipotent, or partly infinite. He is not constructed of a section or segment of being that is then added to other sections or segments to comprise the whole of God. It is not so much that God has attributes but rather that He is His attributes. In simple terms (as distinct from difficult terms) this means that all of God's attributes help define all of His other attributes. For example, when we say God is immutable, we are also saying that His immutability is an eternal immutability, an omnipotent immutability, a holy immutability, a loving immutability, etc. By the same token His love is an immutable love, an eternal love, an omnipotent love, a holy love, etc." (Loved, pp. 6 - 7)

The following section is a brief history of philosophy. If you take the time to grasp the following descriptions, you will be able to better understand the two dominant philosophies of our secular world: Pantheism and Naturalism. Parmenides, argued for *Monism (Mono* = One). There are two branches of monism (what Clive calls *Everythingism*):

(Lewis:) "Thus the Everythingist, if he starts from God, becomes

a Pantheist; there must be nothing that is not God. If he starts from Nature
he becomes a Naturalist; there must be nothing that is not Nature."
(Miracles, p. 301)

(Geisler:) "Parmenides, born circa 515 B.C. argued that all is one, because
to assume that more than one thing exists is absurd. If there were two or
more things, they would have to differ, but the only ways to differ are by
something (being) or by nothing (non-being). However, it is impossible to
differ by nothing, since to differ by nothing (or nonbeing) is just another
way of saying there is no difference at all. And two things cannot differ by
being because being (or existence) is the only thing they have in common- it
is impossible to differ by the very respect in which they are the same.
Hence, Parmenides concluded that it is impossible to have two or more
things. There can be only one being: All is one, and one is all. Thus,
whatever else appears to be does not really exist."

      (Geisler:) "Put in the context of creation, this simply means that
God exists and the world does not; there is a creator, but not really any
creation. Or, at least, the only sense in which there can be said to be a
creation is that it comes out of God the way a dream comes from a mind.
The universe is only the nothing of which God thinks. God is the totality of
all reality, and the non-real about which he thinks and which appears to us,
like zero, does not exist. It is literally nothing."

      (Geisler:) "The famous Hindu philosopher Shankara described the
relation of the world to God, illusion to reality, by the analogy of what
appears to be a snake but on closer examination turns out actually to be a
rope. When we look at the world, what is there is not reality; rather it is
merely an illusion. Likewise when a person looks at himself, what appears
to be (body) is only an illusory manifestation of what really is (soul). And
when one looks into his soul, he discovers that the depth of his soul is really
the depth of the universe: Man is God. To think we are not God is part of
the illusion or dream from which we must awaken. Sooner or later we must
discover that all comes from God, and all is God." (ST 2, pp. 427 - 428
underline is mine)

      Geisler summarizes monism:

      (Geisler:) "There cannot be more than one thing (absolute
Monism), for if there were two things, they would have to differ. For things

to differ, they must differ either by being or by nonbeing. But since being is
that which makes them identical, they cannot differ by being. Nor, on the
other hand, can they differ by nonbeing, for nonbeing is nothing, and to
differ by nothing is not to differ at all. Hence, there cannot be a plurality of
beings (both God and creatures) but only one single indivisible being - a
rigid monism." (ST 1, pp. 21 - 22)

This version of monism is called absolute pantheism since it begins with
the presupposition that there is a god.

There are two ways to try and defeat the brilliance of Parmenides. One
way is to have things differ by non-being, the other is to find a difference in
the beings themselves.

The Atomists, (Leucippus and Democritus, circa 500-370 B.C.)
contended that the principle separating one being (or atom) from another is
absolutely nothing (non-being). They called this the Void. The atoms do not
differ in their essence, but in the space they occupy, so each being occupies a
different space in the Void, and the void is empty space or non-being.
Parmenides would simply point out that to differ by absolutely nothing is to
have absolutely no difference at all. And to have absolutely no difference is
to be absolutely the same. (see ST 1, p. 22)

Plato, with the help of Parmenides, tried to use "relative nonbeing" as the
principle of differentiation. He argued that nonbeing in some way exists. One
being is distinct from another not by what it is, but by what it is not. For
example, the chair is distinguished from everything else in the room in that it
is not the table, the floor, the wall, etc. Parmenides would simply have asked
whether there were any differences in the beings themselves. If there were
not, then he would have insisted that all these beings must be identical. For
the monist there are not many beings but only one. (see ST 1, pp. 22 - 23)

Aristotle argued that there is a plurality of 47 or 55 beings, or unmoved
movers, that are separated from one another in their very being. Parmenides
would ask Aristotle just how simple beings can differ in their very being.
Things composed of form and matter can differ in that THIS particular
matter is different from THAT matter, even though they have the same form.
But how do pure forms (beings) differ from each other? They have no
principle of differentiation. If there is no difference in their being, then their

being is identical. Aristotle was unable to avoid monism. (see ST 1, p. 22 - 23)

Finally, Thomas Aquinas, like Aristotle, sought differences within the beings themselves. Aquinas believed that all finite beings -for example: angels and man- are composed in their very being, while God is an absolutely simple (indivisible) Being, and there can only be one such Being. God is infinite, all creatures are finite. God is pure actuality (Act), all creatures are composed of actuality (act) and potentiality. Hence, finite things differ from God in that they have a limiting potentiality; He does not. Finite things can differ from each other in whether their potentiality is completely actualized (as in angels) or whether it is being progressively actualized (as in humans).

In all creatures their essence (is-ness) is really distinct from their existence (what-ness). In God, on the other hand, His essence and existence are identical. Since God is without all composition, His understanding is not distinct from His essence. Aquinas was not the first to make this distinction, but he was the first to make extensive use of it. Aquinas argues that existence is something other than essence, except in God, whose essence is His existence. Such a being must be one and unique, since multiplication of anything is only possible where there is a difference. Parmenides assumed that being is always understood in the same way, Aquinas saw that being is analogous -- being understood in similar but different ways. (see ST 1, p. 24) The creator is absolutely simple in His being. God cannot become more loving, more powerful, more wise, more righteous, etc. God is in a state of perfection, and since He is perfect and immutable, He is unable to sin. Any attribute that is in the essence of God extends to every other attribute that is in the essence or being of God.

While God is simple, His creation is composed and has potentiality. A tree can be cut down, sawed into boards and made into a table and chairs. The same table and chairs can be cut up and made into a fire. Angels can become demons, or they can learn from the rebellion of Satan and gain an understanding of what happens when one sins. Man changes every day. We grow and age. We learn to think, speak, and do math. We have experiences which change us.

Let us take our ability to reason and look at a few scriptures and see how this actually works in practice:

Genesis 1: 1 - 3 "In the beginning, God created the heavens and the earth. The earth was without form and void, and darkness was over the face of the deep. And the Spirit of God was hovering over the face of the waters. And God said, "Let there be light," and there was light." (ESV)

John 1: 1- 3 "In the beginning was the Word, and the Word was with God, and the Word was God. He was in the beginning with God. All things were made through Him, and without Him was not any thing made that was made." (ESV - Erasmus and Calvin translate Logos as "the Speech" instead of as "the Word" --see Calvin's commentary on John 1)

The first passage shows the tri-unity of God. God (The Father) created, the Spirit of God (The Holy Spirit) was hovering over the face of the waters, and God said (God the Word), "Let there be light." It is the passage in John that identifies the Word of God as Jesus. From these two passages of scripture we get the theology of the "trinity" -- God as three persons. A few years ago I was having a discussion with a Mormon, and he said to me, "You Christians, are so silly. You believe a logical contradiction: that God is three persons in one person." My reply to him was rather simple. I explained to him that if I believed that God was one person and three persons at the same time and in the same sense, he was right that this was a logical contradiction and foolishness. However, the orthodox doctrine of the trinity is that God is three persons in one being (or essence), and that is not logically contradictory.

(Calvin:) "They said that there are three Hypostases, or Subsistence's, or Persons, in the one and simple essence of God." (Commentary on John 1:1)

Using our ability to reason, we read scripture and find the theology that God is described as Father, Word, and Spirit. We use reason to develop two philosophies: The first is that God is three persons in one person. The second is that God is three persons in one being. Using logic, we are able to know the first option is wrong since it violates the law of non-contradiction: (A is not non-A: God is not non-God: God is not the Devil: No two contradictory statements can both be true at the same time and in the same sense.)

Orthodox Christianity uses what is revealed about God in scripture and agrees with the philosophy about God that is not logically contradictory: God is three persons in one being.

=

TERMS AND DEFINITIONS

~

Calvinism: Generally defined as the teachings of Augustine, Luther, and Calvin - which are called Reformed, since they were popularized during the Protestant Reformation in the 1500's. Specifically defined by the Five TULIP Points dealing with Soteriology, which were formulated at the Synod of Dort to rebuke the five points submitted by the followers of Arminius.

Classical Theism: God is simple in His essence, while His creation is composed or complex. Uses Divine Essentialism to determine which attributes of God are essential, or proper, to His essence. Based on the *Summa Theologica* by Thomas Aquinas. See the appendix on philosophy.

Divine Essentialism: Belief that the only attributes of God that are essential to His nature are those attributes that are proper to His nature prior to His creating anything.

Eschatology: Study of Last Things, or End Times.

Exclusivism: Salvation is restricted to those that God chooses to give the gift of faith to; thereby, adopting and regenerating them. God is able to give the gift of faith to all, compelling every person to be saved from eternal damnation, but chooses not to.

Inclusivism: The belief that when it comes to the eternal destination of each person, God will hold each person accountable for the amount of Revelation each individual person received.

Intellectualism: There is a natural law: Something is correct, therefore, God wills it. Also known as Thomism, after Thomas Aquinas.

Natural Law: There is an objective right and wrong which is consistent with the way the universe works.

Reformed: Those that follow the teachings of Augustine, Luther, and Calvin in the areas of Sovereignty, Grace, and Soteriology.

Solecism: An error. Something that is incorrect.

Soteriology: Salvation.

Voluntarism: God is to be conceived of as some form of will: What God wills is correct, because He willed it. Also known as Scotism, after John Duns Scotus.

=

CAST OF CHARACTERS IN CHRONOLOGICAL ORDER

~

Irenaeus: Disciple of Polycarp who was a disciple of the Apostle John. Bishop in what is now Lyon, France. A church father who wrote *Against Heresies*. (Circa: 125 - 202)

Augustine of Hippo: Calvinists consider Augustine to be the theological father of the Reformation. Bishop of Hippo in Algeria, Africa. Author of more than 100 separate titles. (November 13, 354 - August 28, 430)

Aquinas, Thomas: Italian priest of the Catholic Church in the Dominican Order. Author of *Summa Theologica* as well as other books and articles. (1225 - 1274) Philosopher and Theologian in the tradition of Scholasticism. Proponent of Natural theology and father of the Thomistic school of philosophy and theology.

Luther, Martin: Monk and teacher at Wittenberg University in Wittenberg, Germany. Posting of his *95 Theses* credited with sparking the Reformation. Author of numerous articles and books. (1483 - 1546)

Pighius, Albert: Dutch Roman Catholic Theologian. Author of several works against the Reformers. (1490 - 1542)

Calvin, John (French: Calvin, Jean): French theologian who moved to Switzerland following violent uprisings against protestants in France. Best known for his *Institutes of the Christian Religion* and his commentaries on the books of the Bible. (1509 - 1564) Yes, Calvin was Reformed and a Calvinist.

Warfield, Benjamin Breckinridge: Professor of Theology at Princeton Seminary. (1851 - 1921) Calvinist - Reformed.

Chesterton, Gilbert Keith: A prolific English writer and Christian Apologist. (1874 - 1936) Anglican, then converted to Roman Catholicism.

Lewis, Clive Staples: Teacher at Magdalen College in Oxford, England for thirty years. Professor of Medieval and Renaissance English at the University of Cambridge. Author of numerous books. (1898 - 1963) Anglican - Church of England.

Geisler, Norman: Chair of Christian Apologetics at Veritas Evangelical Seminary in Murrieta, CA. Professor at several universities or seminaries for over 40 years. Author of over 50 books and numerous articles. (1932 -) Self described "moderate" Calvinist or Amyraldian.

Sproul, R. C.: Chairman of Ligonier Ministries. Author of over 60 books. (1939 -). Calvinist - Reformed.

Piper, John: Pastor of Bethlehem Baptist Church in Minneapolis, MN. Author of over 10 books. (1946 -) Calvinist - Reformed.

Mohler, Albert: President of Southern Baptist Theological Seminary in Louisville, KY. (1959 -). Calvinist - Reformed.

White, James: Director of Alpha and Omega Ministries in Phoenix, AZ. Author of over 20 books. (1962 -) Calvinist - Reformed.

=

BIBLIOGRAPHY

~

The first section gives the abbreviations used in the text of the book, the author, and title. The second section gives the complete citation for each work:

Abolition: Lewis, C. S. *The Abolition of Man.*

BC: Chesterton, G. K. *The Complete Father Brown Stories: The Blue Cross.*

Bondage: Luther, Martin. *The Bondage of the Will.*

CBF: Geisler, Norman. *Chosen But Free: A Balanced View of Divine Election.*

CBG: Sproul, R. C. *Chosen by God.*

EPG: Calvin, John. *A Treatise On The Eternal Predestination of God.*

ESV: English Standard Version

Five Points: Steele & Thomas. *The Five Points of Calvinism: Defined, Defended, Documented.*

KJV: King James Version

Loved: Sproul, R. C. *Loved by God.*

LTM: Lewis, C. S. *Letters To Malcolm: Chiefly on Prayer.*

MC: Lewis, C. S. *Mere Christianity.*

Miracles: Lewis, C. S. *Miracles.*

NIV: New International Version

NKJV: New King James Version

Perfectionism: Warfield, Benjamin Breckinridge. *Perfectionism.*

Perelandra: Lewis, C. S. *Perelandra.*

PF: White, James. *The Potter's Freedom.*

POP: Lewis, C. S. *The Problem of Pain.*

Reason: Geisler, Norman & Brooks, Ronald M. *Come, Let Us Reason. An Introduction to Logical Thinking.*

SBJ: Lewis, C. S. *Surprised by Joy.*

Silent: Lewis, C. S. *Out of the Silent Planet.*

Strength: Lewis, C. S. *That Hideous Strength.*

ST 1: Geisler, Norman. *Systematic Theology, Volume One.*

ST 2: Geisler, Norman. *Systematic Theology, Volume Two.*

ST 3: Geisler, Norman. *Systematic Theology, Volume Three.*

TGD: Lewis, C. S. *The Great Divorce.*

TLB: Lewis, C. S. *The Last Battle.*

TMN: Lewis, C. S. *The Magician's Nephew.*

Unspoken Sermons: MacDonald, George. *Unspoken Sermons, Series I, II, and III.*

VDT: Lewis, C. S. *The Voyage Of The Dawn Treader.*

WTB: Sproul, R. C. *Willing to Believe.*

Calvin, John. *A Treatise On The Eternal Predestination Of God. (A Defence Of The Secret Providence of God).* Originally published in Geneva, Switzerland in 1552. Translated by Henry Cole in 1856 and titled: *Calvin's Calvinism.*

Chesterton, G. K. *The Complete Father Brown Stories: The Blue Cross.* Wordsworth Editions Limited. 2006. ISBN: 978-1-85326-003-2 Geisler, Norman. *Chosen But Free: A Balanced View of Divine Election.* (Second Edition). Bethany House Publishers. Bloomington, MN. 1999, 2001. ISBN: 0-7642-2521-9

Geisler, Norman & Brooks, Ronald M. *Come, Let Us Reason: An Introduction to Logical Thinking.* Baker Book House. Grand Rapids, MI. 1990, 2002. ISBN: 0-8010-3836-7

Geisler, Norman. *Systematic Theology, Volume One.* Bethany House Publishers. Bloomington, MN. 2002. ISBN: 0-7642-2551-0

Geisler, Norman. *Systematic Theology, Volume Two.* Bethany House Publishers. Bloomington, MN. 2003. ISBN: 0-7642-2552-9

Geisler, Norman. *Systematic Theology, Volume Three.* Bethany House Publishers. Bloomington, MN. 2004. ISBN: 0-7642-2553-7

Heschel, Abraham Joshua. *The Prophets.* Hendrickson Publishers, Inc. Peabody, MA. 2009. ISBN: 978-1-59856-181-4 Copyright 1962 by Abraham J. Heschel.

Lewis, C. S. *Letters To Malcolm: Chiefly On Prayer.* Harcourt, Inc. ISBN: 0I5-602766-6 (pb.) Copyright 1964, 1963, C. S. Lewis Pte. Ltd. Copyright renewed 1992, 1991 by Arthur Owen Barfield.

Lewis, C. S. *The Chronicles of Narnia.* HarperCollins Publishers, New York, NY. ISBN: 0-06-059824-7

The Magician's Nephew. Copyright 1955, C. S. Lewis Pte. Ltd.

The Lion, The Witch And The Wardrobe. Copyright 1950, C. S. Lewis Pte. Ltd.

The Horse and His Boy. Copyright 1954, C. S. Lewis Pte. Ltd.

Prince Caspian. Copyright 1951, C. S. Lewis Pte. Ltd.

The Voyage Of The Dawn Treader. Copyright 1952, C. S. Lewis Pte. Ltd.

The Silver Chair. Copyright 1953, C. S. Lewis Pte. Ltd.

The Last Battle. Copyright 1956, C. S. Lewis Pte. Ltd.

Lewis, C. S. *The Complete C. S. Lewis Signature Classics.* HarperSanFrancisco. ISBN: 0-06-050608-3

 Mere Christianity. Copyright 1952, C. S. Lewis Pte. Ltd.

 The Screwtape Letters. Copyright 1942, C. S. Lewis Pte. Ltd.

 Miracles. Copyright 1947, C. S. Lewis Pte. Ltd.

 The Great Divorce. Copyright 1946, C. S. Lewis Pte. Ltd.

 The Problem of Pain. Copyright 1940, C. S. Lewis Pte. Ltd.

 A Grief Observed. Copyright 1961, C. S. Lewis Pte. Ltd.

 The Abolition of Man. Copyright 1944, C. S. Lewis Pte. Ltd.

Lewis, C. S. *Out of the Silent Planet.* Scribner. New York, NY. 2003. ISBN: 978-0-7432-3490-0 Copyright 1938 by Clive Staples Lewis.

Lewis, C. S. *Perelandra.* Scribner. New York, NY. 2003. ISBN: 978-0-74323491-7 Copyright 1944 by Clive Staples Lewis. Copyright 1972 by Alfred Cecil Harwood and Arthur Owen Barfield.

Lewis, C. S. *That Hideous Strength.* Scribner. New York, NY. 2003. ISBN: 978-0-7432-3492-4 Copyright 1945, 1946 by Clive Staples Lewis. Copyright 1973, 1974 by Alfred Cecil Harwood and Arthur Owen Barfield.

Lewis, C. S. *The Beloved Works of C. S. Lewis: Surprised by Joy: Reflections on the Psalms: The Four Loves: The Business of Heaven.* Inspirational Press. New York, NY. ISBN: 978-0-88486-445-5

 Surprised by Joy, copyright 1986, 1984 by Arthur Owen Barfield.

Luther, Martin. *The Bondage of the Will.* Henry Cole, translation. Baker. 1976.

MacDonald, George. *Unspoken Sermons, Series I, II, and III.* Feather Trail Press.

Piper, John. *The Justification of God.* Baker Book House. Grand Rapids, MI. 1993.

Sproul, R. C. *Chosen by God.* Tyndale House Publishers, Inc. Wheaton, IL. 1986. ISBN: 0-8423-0282-4

Sproul, R. C. *Loved by God.* Word Publishing. Nashville, TN. 2001 ISBN: 08499-1648-8

Sproul, R. C. *Willing to Believe*. Baker Book House. Grand Rapids, MI. 1997.

Steele, David N. & Thomas, Curtis C. *The Five Points of Calvinism: Defined, Defended, Documented*. Presbyterian & Reformed Publishing Co. Phillipsburg, NJ. 1963. ISBN: 0-87552-444-3

Warfield, Benjamin Breckinridge. *Perfectionism*. Presbyterian and Reformed Publishing Company, Philadelphia, PA. 1958.

White, James. *The Potter's Freedom*. Calvary Press Publishing. 2009. ISBN: 1-879737-43-4

=

Brothers, if anyone is caught in any transgression, you who are spiritual should restore him in a spirit of gentleness. Keep watch on yourself, lest you too be tempted. Galatians 6:1 (ESV)

~

Thank You for taking the time to read my book.

Any questions or comments will be appreciated:

~

Jordan Ferrier
10930 Skylane Court
Allendale, MI 49401